Lewis

The Story of an Island

Christine Macdonald

foreword by
Margaret Bennett

acair

For the young people of Lewis,
that they may know what a
colourful coat hangs in the
closet, and that they may
take pride in the wearing of it.

It is good to look at the line of our ancestors down a span of centuries, for there is an unspoken need in all of us to discover our roots. Knowledge of the past gives a freedom, a kind of completeness, which is unique. And yet we cannot live in the past:

"... the paths by which we came into the present can never be traversed again. ... Older forms of culture have provided us with the knowledge, the techniques and the tools necessary for our contemporary civilisation. ... No road into the present need be repudiated and no former way of life forgotten. But all these different pasts, our own and all others, must be treated as precursors."

— Margaret Mead, in *Culture and Commitment*

The publishers would like to thank the following for
permission to reproduce the illustrations:
The Trustees of the National Museums of Scotland
The Royal Commission on Ancient and Historical Monuments of Scotland
Historic Scotland, Executive Agency of the Secretary of State for Scotland
The National Library of Scotland
Mary Evans Picture Library
Stornoway Library
Trixie Schulz

This book was first published by Macdonald Publishers
and printed by Macdonald Printers in 1982

THIS EDITION:
Reprinted by Acair Ltd. in 1998
Printed by ColourBooks Ltd., Dublin.

ISBN 0 86152 184 6

Book and Jacket design by Margaret Anne MacLeod, Acair.

Contents

Note: Spellings of Lewis place names etc. are generally as found on
Ordnance Survey Maps. 1:50 000 second series, sheets 8, 13 and 14.

ACKNOWLEDGEMENTS

I wish to acknowledge the works of W.C. Mackenzie and W.H. Murray, which gave me the incentive to begin. Other works of interest are noted at the end of this book.

I would like to thank Mr Donald MacAulay for help with an early draft of the work and the Ordnance Survey Office, Edinburgh, for details of archaeological finds.

I am grateful to Dr Joanna Close-Brooks, Dr Alison Sheridan for her recent revisions, Mr Ian MacDonald, Professor Derick Thomson and the late Mr Donald MacDonald for advice, corrections and great encouragement. I cannot praise them too highly.

C.M.

FOREWORD

When Skyeman Martin Martin decided to tour all of the Western Isles over three hundred years ago and write his *Description*, he began by explaining why anyone should make such a voyage:

The modern itch after the knowledge of foreign places is so prevalent that the generality of mankind bestow little thought or time upon the place of their nativity. It is become customary in those of quality to travel young into foreign countries whilst they are absolute strangers at home; and many of them, when they return, are only loaded with superficial knowledge as the bare names of famous Libraries, stately edifices, fine statues, curious paintings, late fashions, new dishes, new tunes, new dances, painted beauties and the like.

While this is still true, there are also those who 'travel young' then, having seen those 'foreign countries', come back to their own Island with an even keener sense of appreciation for the wealth of its culture. Martin Martin himself had travelled to Edinburgh, London and beyond before he set out on his Island tour, and although he does not say so, I am convinced that his perception of the Islands benefited from his own youthful travels. So too, in reading Christine Macdonald's account of her own Island, we may sense that her life-long appreciation for its history, archaeology and culture can only have been nurtured by every journey travelled since her school days. Standing back for a time has not only sharpened her focus, but, like so many of us who were privileged to have been educated in Lewis, she has had time to consider that, for many of us, it was easier to access knowledge about the Gallic Wars than any Gaelic War, and we were more likely to hear about the Statue of Liberty than the Statutes of Iona.

Scotland has at last entered a stage when pride in nation, culture, language and heritage has found its own place in our collective consciousness. Thankfully then, Christine Macdonald offers an answer to the new generation asking, "Where can I find out about Lewis?" Her book is especially for the young, yet as I read, I was convinced it was for every age.

When I began to read this book, I felt immediately drawn to sharing it with an elderly friend, Norah Montgomerie who, like Christine (only a generation earlier) showed her deep appreciation of Scottish tradition by writing and illustrating books for the young. And so, in the quietness of her room where she suffered from ill-health, I sat by her bedside and read aloud over several summer afternoons. Her bright eyes and frail voice prompted me to 'go on' if I looked up for too long. Then, quite unexpectedly Norah had another visitor - my son, Martyn, who was devoted to this special lady whose books he loves. Gesturing to me not to interrupt the reading, he slipped into our company.

Norah has now sadly passed on. Much later, I telephoned Martyn to ask for some family advice. "It's Kirsten's birthday tomorrow - what would she like?" Without a moment's hesitation he replied, "Get her that wonderful book about Lewis you were reading to Norah - she'd just love that."

For the young, the not so young, and all ages in between; for people of Lewis and for all who have an interest in it; for everyone who loves tradition and culture, Christine Macdonald has given us a book that can only become more treasured as each year goes by.

Margaret Bennett

1.

There is an island in the Outer Hebrides shaped like an ancient arrow-head pointing north, and here are related wonderful tales of giants, seers, warriors and poets.

That island is Lewis, and upon it to this day are the footprints of these people, and we may find them, if only we know where to look. The sea may be stormy —

The waters will be churning in the stream that never smiles,
Where the Blue Men are splashing round the charmed isles. [1.]

THE LAND

Look closely at the wild, stony, treeless, lochan-strewn landscape. Has it not a bare weathered look about it? Not surprisingly — the rock which you see all around (it is called gneiss) is the oldest rock in the British Isles.

Once the Outer Hebrides were joined to the mainland, but many millions of years ago the Atlantic flooded into the valley of the Minch, and the Outer Hebrides, still all in one piece, took form.

Later, in the Ice Ages, the land was greatly altered. Glaciers hundreds of feet thick hollowed out the lochs and scraped away good soil, while far out in the Atlantic the glaciers cracked, with deafening roars, into icebergs.

Then, as the climate became warmer, the ice very slowly began to melt and form channels, so that the land was divided into various islands. The Outer Hebrides as we know them took shape.

New vegetation began to grow. Seeds of birch and hazel were carried from the mainland on the wind. Sea-birds paused on their travels. Later the reindeer, the wolf, the wildcat — and even the brown bear — made their way through the snow and ice.

THE FIRST PEOPLE

Trees, birds, animals — the scene was now set for people to come. Southern Britain was already settled by Palaeolithic or Old Stone Age people — so called because their tools were made of stone. The first people in Lewis probably arrived in the Mesolithic or Middle Stone Age although no artefacts of the period have yet been found in Lewis, perhaps because they have been lost due to beach erosion. In Scotland this is dated between about 7,000 BC and 3,500 BC.

How can we find out about the first people? They belonged to a time before written records. Yet a vivid picture of their lives is available to us. Many people love to poke about rubbish dumps! Archaeologists certainly do, for mounds of discarded rubbish (they are usually called middens) of these early peoples have been found

EOROPIE
AIRD DELL
ADABROCK
GALSON
BARVAS
SHAWBOST
BRAGAR ARNOL
N. TOLSTA
CARLOWAY
BERNERA
L. Roag
GRESS
VALTOS
STORNOWAY
UIG
CALLANISH
L E W I S
GARRABOST
BRENISH
EYE
PENINSULA
BALALLAN
SCARP
CROMORE
PARK
H A R R I S
TARBERT
L. Seaforth
NORTHTON
RODEL

0   10 miles

10km

and excavated in other areas of western Scotland. And it is from these that we build up a picture of early life.

We know that the first people were few in number and that they were hunter-gatherers, on the move after the deer herds or to areas of good shellfish and other food supplies. Clothed in skins, they fished and hunted with bone harpoons and weapons of deer antlers. Knives and scrapers of flint or quartz fashioned these weapons and also cut flesh, scraped skins and tore limpets from the rocks. Arrow-heads consisted of tiny points of the flint or quartz material.

Later, wild dogs were tamed for the hunt. The *curach* or coracle, a boat made of hide stretched over a light wooden frame, was more suitable for these ocean waters than the dug-out canoe.

The first people lived in small groups, possibly occupying a base camp for most of the year, but also using any temporary shelter they could find, or erect, on their hunting expeditions — usually a cave or a rough skin shelter on the seashore, well clear of all the wild animals which lurked in the undergrowth. Recent reappraisals of this period indicate that the people had their own religious ideas though there are no traces of these for us to see.

Their main essentials were their tools, many of which have been found in western Scotland in recent times. These are the prints which they have left us — the life-and-death tools of their survival.

THE FIRST FARMERS

While Scotland had her hunter-gatherers, the people in the Mediterranean areas had discovered how to grow corn and grind it into meal, to keep domestic animals and to make pottery out of clay. At the same time, their stone tools were ground and polished for greater efficiency, which distinguished them from the earlier implements.

We now move into the Neolithic or New Stone Age, the term which indicates the introduction of these skills, which had spread to much of Britain by about 4,000 BC. There is no doubt that people of this period lived in Lewis, for they have left stone tombs, polished stone axes and pottery. Later Neolithic pottery has been found in Lewis and this is decorated with all-over linear designs almost exclusive to the Hebrides. A great deal of this later pottery has also been recovered in an excavation at Northton, Harris.

Heavy clay pots would have been much too cumbersome and fragile for nomadic hunter-gatherers, who used leather and basketry holders. The people who used the pots were, of course, beginning to settle in one place, in order to tend their domestic animals and crops. It is probable that in Lewis the people remained to a large extent hunter-gatherers also, for the harvest of the hunt and of the sea would have continued to be very favourable. Several flint or quartz arrow-heads of this period have been found.

CHAMBERED CAIRNS

In settled conditions, with more freedom from the daily hunt for food, the people seem to have puzzled greatly about death and an afterlife, for, although their houses were simple — probably small huts of stone and wattle — and their tools still primitive, yet they were painstaking in constructing immense stone burial chambers, which as well as indicating great reverence for their dead, may also have been an assertion to others of their ownership of the land. In Lewis the chambers included those at Callanish and Garrabost — with one of the most impressive in the Outer Hebrides being the cairn of Barpa Langass in North Uist.

The chambered cairn, as it is now known, consisted of a roughly circular or rectangular burial chamber, with a passage leading into it from the entrance and the whole enclosed in a mound of stones. It was a communal burial-place, and used over many years. A large stone, to be removed as necessary to receive the dead, sealed the entrance. Clay pots were included for possible use in the afterlife.

Several stone mace-heads (staffs of office) of this time have been found in Lewis, pointing to ceremony and ritual; and no doubt the chambered cairns became centres for this. The stone tombs, the axes, the arrow-heads and the pottery are permanent monuments of the people who built these intricate burial chambers, and who engaged in the ceremonies and rituals of the time.

THREE LATE NEOLITHIC STONE MACEHEADS, AROUND 2500 BC

2.

STANDING STONES

The great standing stones or megaliths in Lewis were erected in the Late Neolithic or Early Bronze Ages, and this work must have been initiated and supervised by powerful and respected leaders. The placing of the stones shows great engineering skill. Some only two or three feet deep in the ground have nevertheless remained upright for thousands of years.

Mathematicians and astronomers who have tried to discover the purpose of the standing stones have come to the conclusion that some stone circles were used for observing the movements of sun and shadow, in order to build up a calendar to indicate the best time for seed-sowing, harvest and other important events of the farming year. (Marks of Bronze Age ploughing have been found in Lewis.) They may also have been used as lunar observatories, perhaps even for predicting eclipses of the moon, a seemingly magical power for the local seers to display. It is probable that they were also used as places of worship.

The marvellous stone circle and avenue at Callanish was known to the early Greeks as 'the Great Winged Temple of the Northern Isles'. In local Gaelic tradition it is *Teampall na Grèine*, 'The Temple of the Sun', a place where sun worship was once celebrated. In an ancient Lewis custom continued up to fairly recent times, people walked *deiseil* or sunwise (clockwise) round cairns to bring good luck, and round leaders or benefactors as a mark of respect.

There are several other stone circles near Callanish and elsewhere in Lewis, and also single standing stones, the most impressive of which is Clach an Truiseil, nearly 20 feet high and the highest standing stone in Scotland. Perhaps the religion of the Neolithic/Bronze Age island dwellers was directed towards the sky, the moon and sun. The grey stones reaching skywards, and overlooking the setting sun in the west, are their memorial today.

STANDING STONES, CALLANISH, LEWIS

LATE BRONZE AGE HOARD FROM ADABROCK

THE BRONZE AGE

As chambered cairns were going out of use on Lewis, there were people living in eastern Scotland who had the skill of making tools and weapons in copper and in bronze (an alloy of copper and tin). And Lewis also gained this skill from about 2,000 BC.

The introduction of metal had greater significance than just the substitution of one material for another. The skill of stone-working, from a material which was close at hand, was taken very much for granted. But the fact that soft green material (ore) from the earth could be transformed in a roaring furnace to make a shiny bronze knife — that was a most amazing and exciting phenomenon. The technique involved prospecting for ore and smelting and working the material; and often, in addition, exporting it to areas of demand, so that trade developed. Areas of mainland Scotland had copper deposits, tin was imported from Cornwall and bronze ingots from Ireland.

Those who possessed the skill of producing metal may have explained it as magic and enhanced their prestige by keeping the secret to themselves. It is possible that in this way the local bronze-worker also came to be regarded as a magical seer or prophet and was made a leader of the people.

Notable Bronze Age articles of the 8th-7th centuries BC have also been unearthed in Lewis. Fragments of a bronze bowl of Continental type, bronze implements, gold and amber beads and two whetstones have been found at Adabrock, and leaf-shaped bronze swords at Aird Dell. The use of a particular type of bronze sword of this time appears to have been centred on Skye and the Outer Isles, and this points to powerful chiefs with weapons at an advanced stage of development, for these have been called the 'ultimate weapon' of the period. The burial cist of a Bronze Age man was also discovered in 1992 on the headland overlooking Berie Sands, Uig.

BRONZE SWORD FROM NESS, BRONZE AGE

THE IRON AGE

From the 6th century BC iron tools and weapons began to come into use in Britain and would have been in common use in Lewis and elsewhere by about 100 BC. This was a great step forward, for iron was stronger and more plentiful than bronze, which was eventually used mainly for coins, jewellery, helmets and horse-harness fittings, since it could be melted and cast into intricate shapes, while all iron objects had to be wrought (that is, hammered). So great was the demand for iron goods that a flourishing trade soon built up which, as well as ironware, distributed precious metals, cattle, farm produce and slaves. (Before the use of prisons, slavery was the only alternative to killing all prisoners of war.)

DUNS AND BROCHS

The Iron Age was an era of great stone fortification in Lewis. Fortresses called duns (from the Gaelic word *dùn*) seem to have been built over a long period of time, probably from 600 BC to 600 AD, or even later; and about 40 of these have been traced in Lewis. For extra safety many were placed on islets in lochs, where the approach was often by stepping-stones, set in a curve as an advantage in defence. One of these stepping-stones, later named *clach glagain* ('noisy stone') in Gaelic, was balanced in such a way that it made a noise when stepped upon and so gave warning at night. Other islets were joined by massive causeways, and refuge walls against sudden attack were sometimes built across rocky headlands.

Brochs, magnificent fortresses with massive round drystone walls, were erected about the first two centuries AD. Over 500 have been recorded along the coasts of the north and north-west mainland and islands, and they are all so alike that they

Lewis

OBJECTS FROM VARIOUS IRON AGE SITES, INCLUDING GALSON

must have been built during the same period. They can probably best be described as the fortified farmhouses of one social group or extended family. Those in Lewis include *Dùn Chàrlabhaigh*, the well-known and well-preserved broch at Doune Carloway, and ruined ones at Bragar, and near Berie Sands, Uig.

The period of the construction of the brochs coincided with the Roman invasion of Britain. The Romans, however, did not settle northern Scotland, although trading took place, at least to a limited extent, in the early wool trade between the Roman world and the Hebrides. Specialised weaving combs of deer horn, clay loom weights and bone pins, needles and awls of this time have been found in the excavated midden of a stone structure at Galson, telling of this already developing local industry which continues in today's tweeds. (Patterned weave, now called tartan, was known from the 3rd century AD.)

As well as weaving implements, the midden at Galson produced pottery and saddle querns. But from about the 1st century BC/AD the rotary quern came into use in the Highlands. This was a great improvement, in allowing faster production of meal, but it is known that the teeth of early people were worn flat from grit in the meal produced by the querns.

The era of fortification tells of a people who felt threatened, attempting to protect their own rights. What did they fear? New land seekers, the might of Rome, or even neighbouring tribes determined to take over, or raiding in search of goods or slaves? It seems that the fortresses served both as a warning to all comers that the people were ready to defend themselves, and also as a statement to others about the

Dun Carloway

broch owners' high ranking status and power over the local people who occupied and worked simple homesteads. In the later centuries BC these took the form of wheelhouse settlements, in machair areas, as also discovered at the headland overlooking Berie Sands.

Look, then, at the sturdy grey broch. Try to imagine the watchers, who guarded its walls, and their own prestige, with piles of stones for their slings, with great iron swords for close fighting and with sharp and deadly spears. And still today we have many of these prints of the Iron Age — implements of war and of peace.

THE CELTS

The Iron Age peoples of Britain were mainly of Celtic origin. These fierce tribal warriors and cultivators of land had gradually spread into Britain and Ireland from Central Europe. Although successive invasions of other peoples absorbed many of the other Celtic elements, Celtic languages were retained in Ireland, parts of Scotland, Wales and, for a time, in the Isle of Man and Cornwall. Gaelic (Scottish and Irish) and Welsh are both Celtic languages. Lewis is a Gaelic-speaking island, and there a Celtic language lives on.

The Celts were renowned as warriors in all the countries of the Continent in which they travelled and settled. A warrior aristocracy ruled the tribe and competed

15

for dominance with other tribes in the area, fighting fiercely with sword, spear and sling. And they had the gory custom of beheading their enemies and carrying their heads home in triumph. Celtic women were also noted for their fierceness — often, it was said, equalling their men in strength, so that one man, aided by his punching, kicking wife, could overcome several of the enemy. But the status of a woman varied greatly according to the rank of her family and the prosperity of the community.

Gaelic bards sang in praise of their warriors, though nothing was written down until about the 7th century AD. Here is a translation of an 8th century Gaelic poem from Ireland:

> Then Cet said:
> "Conall is welcome,
> Heart of stone,
> Fierce heat of a lynx,
> Brilliance of ice,
> Red strength of wrath,
> Beneath bosom of a warrior
> Who is wound-dealing and battle-victorious.
> Thou, the son of Findchóem, art comparable to me!"
>
> And Conall said:
> "Cet is welcome,
> Cet son of Mágu,
> Place where dwells a champion,
> Heart of ice,
> Tail of a swan,
> Strong chariot-warrior in battle,
> Warlike ocean,
> Lovely eager bull,
> Cet son of Mágu!" [2.]

Religious rites were conducted by the Druids, who were also responsible for educating the young pupil Druids in the oral traditions of the tribe. The Druids were assisted by the seers and bards, who memorised the old poems and folk tales as well as composing new ones. We shall see later how Celtic religious rites and early Gaelic literature and rites made a long-lasting impression on Lewis.

On the Continent, the Celts generally can be defined as a cultural group from about 800 BC, on the evidence of artefacts of the period from Hallstatt in Austria, and further refinement of their culture on the Continent is shown in examples of art and craftwork of about 500 BC from La Tène in Switzerland. An impressive example of Celtic artwork in Britain is the London Battersea shield of about the 1st century BC, the design of which indicates that the level of Celtic art in southern Britain equalled, by then, that of La Tène, and also had its own great individuality, at a time when Continental Celtic culture was in decline under Roman attack.

After the Roman invasion of Britain, it was mainly in Ireland — not itself invaded by the Romans — that the Celtic arts flourished. The National Museum of Ireland in Dublin displays the country's magnificent Celtic treasures. Celtic art is very beautiful, with many flowing, curving lines taken from the shapes of tendrils of plants and lightly engraved circular designs, occasionally highlighted with coloured enamel. Intricate designs were applied to bronze bracelets for arm and wrist, gold torques and bronze collars to be worn around the neck, and brooches with which to fasten the richly dyed woollen cloaks of the warrior princes. Such are the prints they have left us — in an art form of superb beauty.

In the early centuries AD Lewis was the domain of two warrior peoples, at least one of whom, as we shall see, was of Celtic origin.

PICTISH SYMBOL STONE FROM STROME, BENBECULA, LATE 7TH OR 8TH CENTURY

3.

PICTS AND SCOTS

From about 300 AD the Romans gave the name *Picti*, or Picts, to all the tribes beyond the Highland Line, a natural boundary which takes a diagonal line from the Firth of Clyde to the Firth of Forth and north of which the Romans never settled.

About this time the Picts were joined by Irish tribesmen of Celtic origin — the *Scotti*, or Scots — in their fight against the Romans, enemies common to them both. These Scots, who came from Ulster in the north of Ireland, began to settle the west coast.

The language and it is thought the inheritance customs of the Picts differed from those of the Scots. They may have been descendants of the pre-Scots settlers, or possibly a mixture of different peoples. However, they lived in contact with the Scots long enough to assimilate much of their way of life. Lewis was probably still partly Pictish in the 7th-8th centuries AD, for Pictish symbol stones and an ogam-inscribed bone knife-handle of about this time have been found in the Outer Hebrides. Unfortunately, Pictish writing, although in a form of Irish script known as ogam, cannot yet be fully deciphered. The symbol stones are works of great craftsmanship and beauty, depicting animals, birds, fish and horsemen and warriors as well as figurative shapes such as circles, crescents and arches.

The inheritance customs of the Picts were thought to include succession through the mother rather than through the father. Women, however, did not rule. But authority was given to men who were brothers — mother's brothers, mother's mother's brothers and so on. Although a queen may rule with absolute power, women in general in society have not held authority over men, and descent through the father has been a much more common rule of succession. Certainly, descent through the mother may have led to conflict between a woman's husband and her brothers over the control of the woman and her children. The system may have been responsible, in this way, for weakening the unity of the Picts, and it may also have enabled Kenneth mac Alpin, King of Scots, to inherit the Pictish kingdom.

After many years of fighting among themselves, the Picts and Scots were united under Kenneth mac Alpin about 843 AD and forced into alliance against the Norsemen, who had seized the whole of the Hebrides by the middle of the 9th century AD. But eventually the Scots dominated, with their kings ruling and the Scots giving their name to the entire country, and the individuality of the Picts was absorbed and almost entirely lost. Virtually all that now remains are the stones with Pictish symbols of unknown meaning upon them, some of which, as we have noted, have been found in the Outer Hebrides.

As we have seen, the Gaelic-speaking Scots from Ireland had entered the west of the country to which they were to give their name from Dalriada, a province of what is now Antrim. From about 500 AD they were established in Argyll (from *Oirthir Gaidheal*, 'The Coast of the Gael' — *Earra-Ghaidheal* in modern Gaelic), and from this new Kingdom of Dalriada they made their expansion at the expense of the Picts.

The Scots certainly brought their own Gaelic culture — arts, crafts, literature and customs — to Lewis. Among these customs very much apparent in Lewis up to very recent times were those connected with the old Celtic year, which was divided into four parts, each preceded by a religious festival.

February 1st was Imbolc, which is though to have involved prayers for the ewes coming into milk. May 1st was Beltane (modern Gaelic Bealltainn), when fires were lit on hilltops and the cattle driven between them to protect them from disease the following year. This rite, intermingling with Christianity, was continued in Lewis up to the 18th century:

Bless, O threefold true and bountiful...
Everything within my dwelling or in my possession,
All kine and crops, all flocks and corn,
From Hallow Eve to Beltane Eve,
With goodly progress and gentle blessing,
From sea to sea and every river mouth,
From wave to wave and base of waterfall. [3.]

August 1st was Lughnasa, with prayers being said for the first ripe ears of corn and a good harvest, and great feasts were held for two weeks before and after. November 1st was Samhain, the beginning of the Celtic year, and a rite was practised on the preceding night (now Halloween, or *Oidhche Shamhna* in modern Gaelic) which sought the protection of the gods in the year ahead.

In a Samhain ritual carried out at Eoropie, until it was stamped out by Presbyterianism in the 17th century, an offering was made to the sea-god Shony, and there were prayers that he might supply a good stock of seaweed as fertiliser for the following year's crops. Festivals were later held on the Quarter days of the Scottish year: Candlemas, February 2nd; Whitsunday, formerly moveable, now May 15th; Lammas, August 1st; and Martinmas, November 11th.

As well as the various gods of nature, each tribe had its own individual god, who was thought of as the ancestor of the people. Other gods controlled every aspect of life. The early Scots, like other peoples, carefully observed nature and made decisions according to the signs that they read in it, with omens being seen in bird flight and bird calls, with taboos against eating certain animals, many sacrifices to placate the gods (which might include human sacrifice) and great celebrations to thank a generous god for a good harvest or victory over other tribes.

Lewis

And so the many small superstitions held by the people of the Hebrides are perhaps not so surprising in the light of the staunchly held beliefs of these early Celtic islanders:

I heard the cuckoo with no food in my stomach,
I heard the stock-dove on the top of the tree,
I heard the sweet singer in the copse beyond,
And I heard the screech of the owl of the night.

I saw the lamb with his back to me,
I saw the snail on the bare flagstone,
I saw the foal with his rump to me,
I saw the wheatear on a dyke of holes,
I saw the snipe while sitting bent,
And I foresaw that the year would not
Go well with me. [4.]

But of course the main imprint which the early Scots left in Lewis was the Gaelic language, which gives Lewis and other Highland areas their great individuality today — for here, in contrast to the rest of Britain, Gaelic is the living language of the people. And we shall see later that it has continued to survive against great odds.

4.

EARLY LITERATURE

The society of the early Scots was a heroic society with a great love of epic poetry, and their *fileda* (modern Gaelic *filidhean*) or poets brought with them the tales and poems of the Gaels, and there was a common literary tradition between the two Gaelic-speaking areas of Ireland and Scotland which was to last until the 17th century. The same stories, for example, turned up, with variations, in both countries again and again.

The oldest stories, set well before the Christian era, are mythical tales about the *Fir Bolg*, who were earth powers, or possibly the pre-Celtic peoples; the *Tuatha Dé Danann*, the higher gods of summer, of light, of music and the arts; and the Fomorians, who were sea rovers and gods of misrule and death. The Fir Bolg were overcome by the Tuatha Dé Danann, and both of them were attacked by the Fomorians. When the Gaelic race arrived, the Tuatha Dé Danann, it was said, first used magical powers over them, but then became resigned to their occupying the land and withdrew to the fairy mounds, from which they watched over the people.

Stories set in the 1st century AD relate the adventures of the hero Cù Chulainn (or Cuchuilin), a famous warrior and champion of Ulster who was said to have trained in the art of combat on the Island of Skye. In the story of a battle against Maeve, the warrior Queen of Connacht, Ferdia, Cù Chulainn's friend, goes to her aid, for he is the only one who can match the champion. They meet at a ford and battle fiercely for four days, and then Ferdia is killed. Weak from his wounds, Cù Chulainn grieves for the death of his friend:

> All play, all sport,
> until Ferdia came to the ford.
> Misery! a pillar of gold
> I have levelled in the ford,
> the bull of the tribe-herd,
> braver than any man...
>
> All play, all sport,
> until Ferdia came to the ford.
> I thought beloved Ferdia
> would live forever after me;
> — yesterday, a mountainside;
> today, nothing but a shade. [5.]

The themes are essentially tragic. Mistakenly killing his own son, Cù Chulainn is himself slain in combat. And there is the sad tale of Deirdre, who falls in love with Naoise. But Conchobar, King of Ulster, wishes Deirdre for himself. The lovers flee to

Scotland, but when they are later persuaded to return, Naoise is killed by Conchobar and Deirdre taken captive. Distraught with grief, she flings herself from a chariot.

The next stories, set about 300 AD, are about Fionn MacCumhaill, the famous warrior leader of the Fians or Fèinn, soldiers of the King of Ireland who sail off in their galleys to great adventures in the Hebrides. Fionn's son Ossian is a poet and his grandson Oscar a great warrior. These characters may have been based on real historical figures, but if they are their stories have certainly been much embellished.

Brave and chivalrous, fearless in battle, the Fians often had to deal with giants, dragons and monsters. It is said that once, in Lewis, a great open-mouthed monster lunged towards Oscar. He immediately jumped into the monster's mouth, then cut his way out with his knife, killing it!

Oscar is also said to have slain a famous Lewis giant, Cuitheach or Kuoch MacNuaran, who ruled over Uig. One of his brothers, Dearg, ruled over Carloway. Determined to avenge his brother's death, Dearg followed the Fians to Skye, where he engaged one of their best warriors in combat and fought bravely before he too was killed. Dearg was buried in Skye and Kuoch in Uig, where there is said to be a grave 14 feet long marked by two stones at its head and foot.

Later, Oscar himself was killed in battle, and Ossian, his father, roamed the shores in great melancholy. Here he met a beautiful young girl, Niamh, daughter of the King of Youth, and they sailed off together to the mystical islands far beyond the Hebrides called *Tìr nan Og*, Land of Eternal Youth. When Ossian left Tìr nan Og and returned to Ireland he found Fionn and his warriors long dead, and St Patrick in power. Sadly he composed a poem in honour of Fionn:

A poet he was, and a prince, a king over every king;
Fionn, princely lord of the Fian, was a chief over every land.

A champion great and swift, nimble on a battlefield;
a hawk bright and wise, a sage in every art. ...

Sad am I now that the leader of hundreds is dead;
I am the tree a-tremble, I am a shower after death. ...

A noble man was Fionn. ... [6.]

Many of the stories were later re-written, in a more Christian vein, by monks; but after the Reformation in Scotland the clergy discouraged this folklore for its paganism or Romanism, and it partly disappeared as a living influence among the Highland people. But modern writers have shown great interest in these colourful legends; for example, the notable author of children's books, Rosemary Sutcliffe, has written *The Hound of Ulster* about Cù Chulainn and *The High Deeds of Finn McCool* about Fionn.

EARLY CHRISTIANITY

St Ninian (in the 5th century) and Calum Cille or St Columba (in the 6th century) first brought Christianity to the Picts and Scots, Columba founding the religious centre of Iona about 563 AD. From these missions Christian communities were formed at centres of population, and Christian hermits in search of seclusion found refuge on remote islets in the Hebrides.

In the chaos after Rome and its western empire was overrun by Huns, Goths and Vandals, the Celtic Church maintained its course independent of Rome. But when communications with the Roman Church re-opened, the Celtic Church agreed, after the Synod of Whitby about 664 AD, to accept the authority of Rome. What is perhaps the most beautiful illuminated book in the world, the Book of Kells, is thought to have been begun in Iona, although it has taken its name from the Abbey of Kells in County Meath in Ireland where it was completed. It is from about the 8th century AD and of late Celtic period style.

In the late 8th century the Vikings quelled, but did not dispel, Christianity. Although the monasteries were forced to close, monks took refuge on small islands such as North Rona, near Lewis, where there is a ruined hermitage dating from about this time. By the middle of the 9th century, however, they began to gather again in communities known as Culdees (from the Gaelic *Céili Dé* — 'Companions of God') which kept the faith alive in the following centuries.

Although there is no proof that Columba ever visited Lewis, it is likely that one of his followers did; and, according to tradition, St Columba's Church at Eye was built on the site of a cell of the Celtic St Catan of the 6th or 7th century. There is also an old church of the same name on an island near Cromore, Lochs.

Further evidence pointing to early Christianity in Lewis is found at the long-cist cemetery at Galson. This is thought to be among the earliest types of Christian burial ground, and it is similar to a large number in the Lothians, one of which has a memorial stone, presumably Christian, and is dated not later than the 6th century AD.

Another significant church is that of St Molua at Europie. Certain aspects of the church, now restored, suggest it may have been built in the early 16th century, although possibly on the site of an earlier cell.

5.

THE VIKINGS

Towards the end of the 8th century the fierce raiders known as the Norsemen or Vikings began to plunder Britain from the Scandinavian countries — Norway, Sweden and Denmark. The Hebrides fared badly, being often raided on the Vikings' path south and again on their return north, as well as being used as a base for raids elsewhere:

> For murder and for mauling
> They are come,
> For howling and for hazard
> They are come,
> For pillage and for plunder
> In rain and in wind
> To lift the calving kine
> They are come upon us. [7]

In the 9th century, because of overpopulation in Scandinavia, Norse settlers came in search of land, forcing out the inhabitants or conquering and enslaving them. In Ireland and southern Britain independence was maintained only after great strife, but in the east, middle and north of England, in parts of Wales and in western and northern Scotland, the Norsemen became dominant.

The islands of the Hebrides were so completely overcome that they were called *Innse Gall* or 'Islands of the Foreigners' — a name that has persisted in Gaelic to this day. Norsemen from Lewis fought the Irish at the battle of Clontarf outside Dublin in 1014, when Brian Boroimhe or Boru, High King of Ireland, defeated an army of 20,000 Norsemen and crushed the power of the Norse as a ruling force in Ireland. In Lewis a new race of mixed Celtic and Norse ancestry came into being.

At the end of the 11th century, attempts were made to break away from the power of Norway, and a new title, 'King of Man and the Isles', was adopted. King Magnus III of Norway came to Lewis with a large fleet, to put down the rebellion. The people were forced to flee among the hills or take to sea in their boats, as raiding parties burned everything in their path, and gained victory. Uist, Skye, Mull, Tiree and the Isle of Man were then also attacked. The holy Island of Iona was not raided on this occasion, as Magnus III regarded himself as a Christian. Norway retained the northern Hebrides but the King of Man and the Isles was soon able to regain control of the southern islands.

The Norsemen were rugged and violent in conquest, yet they were respectful towards their own women, seeking their advice in many matters. Women held property of their own and legally shared the property of any marriage. Divorce was allowed for unfaithfulness or ill-treatment, but separation was only by mutual agreement of both husband and wife, with penalties if this rule was broken.

The Norse had their own gods, chief of whom was Odin. Odin, his son Thor, god of Thunder, and his band of hero gods were regarded as lords of the earth. They lived in a huge palace with its great hall, Valhalla, into which entered the spirits of the men slain in battle. From there they guarded the people from the evil giants who lived in the mountains of the north, spending the days in strenuous combat and the nights in feasts of mead and boar's meat.

Every Norseman eagerly looked forward to entering Valhalla, and the Valkyries, fierce maidens on winged horses, came to carry the spirits of the slain there in triumph. But legend stated that one day even Valhalla would fade away, to be replaced by a new order. And so it was. Most Norsemen were converted to Christianity by 1000 AD, and possibly before that in the Hebrides.

The Norsemen were brilliant seamen, and designed and built swift vessels called longships. They loved their ships, carved representations of them on stones and wrote poems in their praise, giving them such names as 'Deer of the Sea' and 'Raven of the Wind'. The swiftness of the longships and the Norse skill in handling them did much to invoke terror. In an instant, it seemed, they might appear out of nowhere to plunder, wielding terrifying axes, swords and daggers.

Norse chiefs were often buried in their ships, along with their most prized possessions, although burning on funeral pyres was also practised. No ship's burials have yet been found in Lewis, but other Viking burials include a woman's grave found at Valtos which contained two Norse oval brooches, which must have been pinned to the straps of her dress, a Celtic brooch to fasten a cloak, and other trinkets of the 9th century. Another Viking grave, found by chance in Uig, was of a woman buried with two gilded brooches, a necklace of glass beads, a bronze belt buckle and various other personal possessions including a bone comb, a needle in a needlecase, a whetstone, an iron knife and an iron sickle. Irish (Celtic) brooches, the booty of plunder, are often found in Norse graves.

Another Norse find in Lewis was made at Dibidail Moss, Barvas Parish, and it consisted of a small hoard of silver armlets of a type called 'ring-money', and probably used as such, and silver finger rings of the 10th century. The Norse, too, had their own individual art forms, with delicate ornamentation and craft work of great skill and beauty.

The most famous Norse find in Lewis must certainly be the Scandinavian walrus ivory chessmen found in an Uig sand dune in 1831. All are beautifully carved, with amazingly realistic expressions on their faces. Some of the rooks or warders are portrayed as foot-soldiers biting the top of their shields in gruesome fury and building up their wrath against the enemy. There are four sets, none complete. They have been dated by their costumes to about the middle of the 12th century, and they are among the oldest chess sets in Europe.

Lewis

Lewis chess men, 12th century, carved from walrus ivory

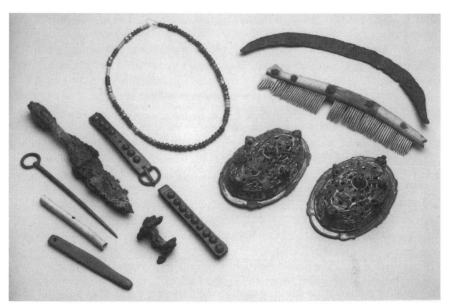

Objects from a norsewoman's grave at valtos

However, the main imprint of the Norse in Lewis is to be found in the names of places and topographical features. For example, *stadhr*, meaning 'dwelling-place' or 'farm', is to be found (in an adapted form) in the final part of such names as Tolstadh (anglicised as Tolsta) and Mangarstadh (Mangersta). *Setr*, meaning 'shieling', appears in the place-names Grimseadar and Linseadar (Grimshader and Lynshader), and it forms the whole name in Siadar (Shader). *Bolstadhr*, referring to the main farm of the village, becomes 'bost' in Crosabost and Siabost (taken into English as Crossbost and Shawbost).

All Lewis was held by the Norse for over four centuries, but much of the way of life of the Gaelic Scots survived to absorb theirs, so that now the era of the Norsemen might never have been — except, that is, for their indomitable spirit, which was handed down to their Lewis descendants.

So far we have seen successive waves of new discoveries, ideas and culture coming to Lewis. The view that the prehistory of the Highlands was only a much later and poorer copy of southern Britain is not true, certainly not up to the Iron Age.

Areas accessible by sea received new ideas early, and the Hebrides were favourably placed for contact with the megalith-builders and metal-workers of Ireland. Excavations in North Uist, for example, show continuous occupation of a site (The Udal) from Late Neolithic times until the 19th century. And it is probable that the early, intrepid Lewis settlers voyaged in their curachs on favourable Atlantic tidal currents while areas of the mainland remained difficult of access and uninhabited.

However, a gradual deterioration in climate by the beginning of the Iron Age made the Hebrides less favoured in this respect than further south. Together with tree felling since Neolithic times, this encouraged the spread of peat and moss, so that cultivation became more difficult and dependence on cattle increased. The Hebrides were untouched by the influence of Rome, and in the long term the Norse left little impression. It was the way of life of the Gaelic Scots, their language and literature that Lewis was to retain.

6.

THE CLANS

The 12th century was a period of unrest, as the Scots attempted to reclaim the Norse-held territory by force. This was the era of the great Somerled, who won many victories over the Norse before being assassinated in 1164. But Scots power was established, and continued with his successors in the southern Hebrides, where the House of Islay became dominant. One of Somerled's successors was a grandson named Domnall (modern Scottish Gaelic *Dòmhnall*) or Donald, whose heirs were called Macdonald (son of Donald); in this way, in the 13th century, were the first clans formed.

The final defeat of the Norse took place at Largs in 1263 and the territory held by them was ceded to the Crown of Scotland by the Treaty of Perth of 1266, but local strife continued for many years. This was overcome in Lewis by the powerful mainland Earldom of Ross, which was then granted Lewis as a reward.

The House of Islay successors of Somerled took control of the other islands. Later, Macdonald of Islay also took control of Lewis and gave himself the grand title of *Tighearna nan Eilean* — 'Lord of the Isles'. And for several centuries Lewis was caught up in the power struggles of the Lords of the Isles and their conspiracies with England.

The most powerful of the early clan chiefs in Lewis were the Macleod Barons, who were descended from the Norse Olaf the Black, King of Man and the Isles. The Macleods became vassals, or soldiers in the service, of the Macdonald Lord of the Isles. Two other notable early Lewis clans were the Macaulays of Uig and the Morisons of Ness, who from as early as the 14th century were in a constant state of feud with each other.

The word 'clan' comes from the Gaelic *clann*, meaning 'children'. This was a group of people with a chief, usually related to them, who banded together for survival (especially to get winter meat) and as a social unit. At first the chiefs were elected by the people, though often from the kinsmen of the old chief, but later the office became hereditary, passing to the male heirs. And though all land and property invested in the chief belonged to the people, there was a tendency for the chiefs to take over the communal property for the benefit of their own families, and to demand services which later became rents, in kind or in money. The later tacksmen were relatives or supporters of the chief, who granted them land at a tack or rent, and they in turn sub-let to the people.

The clans were divided in ranks downwards, from the chief and his relatives to the fighting men and workers on the land, though much of the burden of agriculture fell on the women of the lower ranks. Like the Norse women, the women of the clans were very much respected and their status was high.

The clan chief held a position of great eminence, and he was surrounded by much pomp and ceremony. Each one had his own personal retinue, which was ferried around in proud ships called galleys, and consisted of:

the chief house steward and his men, the bard, the seannachie, the harper and his gillie, the piper and his gillie, the keeper of the sporran, the flag bearer, the big youth, the immediate body man, the cup bearer, the watcher, the huntsman, the fordman, the debater, the luggageman and the jester or clown. [8.]

Hospitality, which was extremely generous, was governed by strict rules of what was fitting, and eventually became a serious drain on the people's resources. Clan justice was conducted by the brieves. From early clan times in Lewis this office of hereditary judge or brieve (from the Gaelic word *britheamh*) belonged to the chief of Clan Morison, whose residence was at Habost, Ness. The brieves were unsparing in doling out judgement according to their own local code. Fines of cattle were imposed for most offences, but the sentence for serious crimes was death by means of the pit or gallows — the pit for drowning women and the gallows for hanging men.

According to tradition, ships wrecked or beached became the lawful prize of the inhabitants of that shore; and Lewis became known as a nest of pirates, to be avoided by shipping at all costs. However, the relatively peaceable attitude of many of the chiefs is shown in the custom of placing *buannaichean*, or buffer watch-dogs (really hench-men of the chief), between clans which were constantly feuding.

In this way, the Macleods settled Macdonalds and Macphails along the west coast to act as a buffer between the Macaulays of Uig and the Morisons of Ness, to prevent incursions by raiding parties across this neutral territory. The buffer watch-dogs were paid in kind for their services by the chief, and in this way some attempt was made to control unruly subjects.

But feuding was almost a way of life. Here is an example of how a feud might develop. Before being accepted as a leader of the clan, every heir or young chieftain was obliged to prove his bravery in a public test. This usually took the form of a raid upon a neighbouring clan against which some grudge was held, and the stealing of its cattle. The clan suffering the loss would immediately set off in pursuit, and a fight to the death might be provoked, which would give further cause for feuding.

Although the early Lewis clans were extremely warlike, they did not, on the whole, fight for glory or for love of war, but because of feuds or for economic reasons. The clans bordering the Lowlands could gain supplies by raids to the south, but in Lewis neighbouring clans were more likely to engage each other in struggles over land and cattle, because land meant power and cattle meant wealth. In addition to this private strife, however, the clans were frequently summoned to fight for the king — by means of a *crann-tàra* or fiery cross, one end of which was set alight, with a cloth of white linen stained with blood being hung from the other. As soon as this was sighted the fighting men seized their weapons and hurried to the rallying point.

Many of the Mackenzie Earls of Seaforth (who took control of Lewis from the Macleod Barons in 1610) were staunch Jacobites, and Lewismen were often drawn into that struggle also. So greatly did the Seaforths love the Stewarts that they spent all their wealth in the Jacobite cause, until finally Kenneth Mackenzie, Baron Fortrose, decided against coming out for Charles Edward Stewart — Bonnie Prince Charlie — in the ill-fated 1745 Rising.

The clan weapons consisted of a huge two handed sword, the claymore (from the Gaelic *claidheamh mòr* — 'great sword'), a dirk and a round shield made of wood covered with hide and with a central spike. Some also carried the terrifying Lochaber axe and, in later times, pistols, muskets and the basket-hilted broadsword. A poem of incitement to battle was often composed by the bard. A translation follows of part of a Gaelic poem of incitement to the Macdonalds before the Battle of Harlaw in 1411.

BASKET-HILTED BROADSWORD FROM C. 1730,
POSSIBLY MADE BY JOHN ALLEN OF STIRLING

DIRKS WITH CARVED WOODEN HILTS, 18TH CENTURY

LATE 17TH-CENTURY TARGE

O children of Conn, remember
hardihood in time of battle:
be watchful, be daring,
be dextrous, winning renown;
be vigorous, pre-eminent;
be strong, nursing your wrath;
be stout, be brave,
be valiant, triumphant. [9.]

When we see the old weapons on display we can imagine the dauntless clansmen, charging into battle with unquestioned bravery. Nevertheless, we are glad that such bloodshed is no longer part of Highland life, and we sympathise with these countries where warfare rages.

7.

THE MACLEOD BARONS OF LEWIS

LEOD, *1st Baron of Lewis (13th c.)*
Leod was a son of the Norse Olaf the Black, King of Man and the Isles. He gained lands in Lewis from his father; in Dunvegan, Skye, by marrying the heiress; and in Harris from his foster-father. His son Tormod inherited Harris and Dunvegan, and his son Torquil inherited Lewis.

TORQUIL, *2nd Baron of Lewis (13th-14th c.)*
Torquil protected his rights by marrying Dorothea, daughter of the Earl of Ross, overlord of Lewis. This was the time of William Wallace and Robert the Bruce, and the struggle for the throne of Scotland after the death of the Maid of Norway. No doubt Lewismen under the leadership of the Earl of Ross, staunch supporter of Robert the Bruce, fought for their King in the victory at Bannockburn in 1314.

TORMOD, *3rd Baron of Lewis (14th c.)*
During this time Chief John Macdonald of Islay gained possession of Lewis, and before long he ruled an area from the Butt of Lewis to Kintyre. He acquired for himself the grand title of Lord of the Isles, and the Macleod Barons became his vassals, or soldiers in his service.

TORQUIL, *4th Baron of Lewis (14th c.)*
The Earldom of Ross competed with the Lords of the Isles for power in the Highlands, and Countess Euphemia of Ross, who was married to the notorious Wolf of Badenoch, gained possession of Lewis. The Wolf, Alexander Stewart, a son of King Robert II, led a reign of terror from his Highland stronghold at Badenoch, and burned down Elgin Cathedral. Torquil Macleod gained lands in Sutherland by marrying the heiress, Margaret Macnicol — some say, by kidnapping her first.

RODERICK, *5th Baron of Lewis (15th c.)*
The year 1411 saw the terrible slaughter of the Battle of Harlaw, Aberdeenshire, between the Macdonald Lord of the Isles, whose daughter Margaret was married to Roderick, (with the promise of help from England), and the forces of the Regent Albany in a dispute over the Earldom of Ross. The larger part of the Macdonald army consisted of men from the Hebrides, including Chief Roderick, his sons and his clansmen. Although the bloodshed was so great that the battle was given the name 'Red Harlaw' the result was indecisive.

TORQUIL, *6th Baron of Lewis (15th c.)*
Torquil Macleod and his brother Tormod, with two companions, were said to have been the first out into the battlefield of Harlaw; though the Macleod brothers survived, both their companions were killed. Torquil later held the office of Magistrate of Trotternish in Skye.

RODERICK, *7th Baron of Lewis (15th c.)*
The power struggles of the Lords of the Isles continued during the period of Roderick; but now the Macdonald ranks split, as Angus, son of John, 4th Lord of the Isles, battled against his own father. Most of the Macdonalds supported the son, but the other island clansmen, including the Macleods of Lewis, were on the side of the father. But John of the Isles was defeated, and Roderick's own son and heir, by his first wife Margaret Macleod of Harris, was killed at the Battle of Bloody Bay, near Tobermory. Roderick's second wife was Agnes MacKenzie of Kintail and their son Torquil succeeded to the title.

LATE MEDIEVAL SCULPTURED MONUMENTS
An effigy in St Columba's church at Eye is thought to be that of Chief Roderick Macleod of the 15th century. He is wearing the quilted tunic, pointed helmet and chain mail of the period.

An ornate grave slab in the church is that of his daughter Margaret. This stone, now much worn, is lavishly decorated with leaf-like interlacing and animal designs, and is an example of a distinctive West Highland native art which flourished in Iona and other areas of the West Highlands and Islands at this time.

It is thought that Margaret was the mother of the last Abbot of Iona; if she was, that could account for her tomb. But over 600 of these magnificent late medieval sculptured monuments are in existence or on record, pointing to a period of great artistic achievement in the Hebrides at that time. This type of decoration was also applied to metal, bone and wood, and probably also to leatherwork and embroidery; but it is mainly the richly carved stone crosses and grave slabs, many bearing the effigies of chiefs and ecclesiastics, which survive. There are also fine examples at Rodel, Harris.

TORQUIL, *8th Baron of Lewis (15th-16th c.)*
The Lord of the Isles turned again to England for support and, in 1493, King James IV of Scotland declared the title of Lord of the Isles forfeit. It is now that we have the first mention of the old Stornoway Castle, the Macleod fortress which stood on a rocky islet protecting the inner harbour at Stornoway. For it was here that Torquil, whose second wife was a Macdonald of Islay, gave refuge to Donald Dubh MacDonald, in his desperate efforts to retrieve by force his family's right to the title of Lord of the Isles. Stornoway Castle was besieged and Lewis overrun by Crown troops seeking Macdonald, and Torquil's estates were also forfeited to the Crown.

EFFIGY OF A WEST HIGHLAND
WARRIOR, POSSIBLY RODERICK
MACLEOD OF LEWIS, A 15TH
CENTURY CHIEF, EYE CHURCH

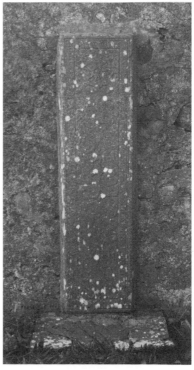

CARVED GRAVE SLAB OF MARGARET
MACLEOD, DAUGHTER OF CHIEF
RODERICK MACLEOD, EYE CHURCH

Tomb of alexander macleod of dunvegan, st clement's church,
rodel, harris

MALCOLM, *9th Baron of Lewis (16th c.)*

The estates were returned to Torquil's brother Malcolm, who was married to Christina Urquhart of Cromarty, and his son — the rightful heir — excluded. Donald Dubh was imprisoned in Stirling Castle, but he later escaped; and strife continued for many years over claims to the Lordship of the Isles, after the death of James IV at Flodden in 1513 and during the reign of James V and the Regency which followed. Long divided in loyalty between the Macdonalds and the Crown, the Macleods nonetheless fought for the King at Flodden, for they admired the courage of James IV; and it is said that, like themselves, he spoke the Gaelic language (having learned it as part of his policy of conciliation).

RODERICK, *10th Baron of Lewis (16th c.)*

The Macdonalds never retrieved the Lordship of the Isles and their power waned. Despite the strife the Lords of the Isles caused and their conspiracies with England, their fall had a detrimental effect on the Hebrides. They had provided periods of stability, in which the arts flourished and churches were built and generously endowed. Now the chiefs, left without a strong and respected overlord, fell to feuding, so that it was every clan for itself. In Lewis, Chief Roderick Macleod divorced his wife Janet Mackenzie of Kintail and disinherited their son (though it must be stated that she had already eloped with her husband's nephew), and this caused a long war over the succession which involved all the other island clans. But Roderick held on to all his possessions (mainly by cutting off the heads of any who opposed him) until he died at the age of 95! Meanwhile, on the mainland two powerful families, the Mackenzies and the Campbells, were profiting from the downfall of the Macdonalds and taking control.

THE FIFE ADVENTURERS

Lewis was in a state of anarchy. King James VI, in need of money, decided he had good enough excuse to take over the island; and he sent a group from the Lowlands, the Fife Adventurers, to go and settle Lewis. They arrived in the winter of 1598 and, after fending off several attacks by the Macleods, they built a settlement on South Beach, Stornoway. But severe conditions, disease and lack of provisions struck hard, and after many Macleod attacks, over several years, the settlers abandoned the attempt and left the island.

STORNOWAY — BURGH OF BARONY

In 1607, before the final defeat, James VI (now also James I of England), granted Stornoway a Charter to become a burgh of barony for the Adventurers, Sir James Elphinstone (Lord Balmerino), Sir James Spens and Sir George Hay. A burgh of barony received the privilege of holding certain fairs and markets, although it was not allowed to deal in foreign trade, which was controlled by the royal burghs.

THE BOND AND STATUTES OF IONA

After his lack of success by colonisation, James VI and I decided to try a different method in an effort to curb the unruly chiefs and their subjects, and in 1609 the Bond and Statutes of Iona were passed. Although slow to take effect, they pointed the way to some improvement in the lives of the islanders; but in seeking to weaken the power of the Gaelic bards and give prestige to Lowland education, they had a detrimental effect on the Gaelic language.

Firearms, poems of incitement to battle, and the import of wine were to be banned, and the chief's retinue was to be cut. Sorners (those demanding hospitality as a right) were to be dealt with as thieves, and inns were to be established to relieve the people of the burden of compulsory hospitality. The eldest sons of the more prosperous were to be sent to Lowland schools, and the Church and clergy supported and maintained.

The state of civil war in Lewis was almost at an end. In 1610 Kenneth Mackenzie of Kintail, Ross-shire, who was involved by marriage with the Macleods and who had long been planning a takeover, bought the Charter rights to Lewis from the Fife Adventurers and was given the right to use 'fire and sword' to reduce the power of the Macleods.

Their leader, Neil Macleod, took refuge with his followers on the island of Berisay in Loch Roag, a sea loch on the west of Lewis. It was a harsh existence on this small rock in the wild Atlantic, and when they realised there was no further hope for their cause they surrendered.

Neil Macleod was taken, and he was hanged in Edinburgh in 1613. The state of war in Lewis soon ended, and the line of the Macleod Barons of Lewis also ended when all the rightful successors died without male heirs and the representation passed to the Macleods of Raasay, Skye.

From the 13th century to the early 17th century the Macleod Barons most decidedly left their mark on Lewis. They were a family of consequence and eminence, and their loyalty to the Macdonalds was understandable, despite the conspiracies with England, for the Lords of the Isles were regarded as kings in the territories under their sway.

Nothing now remains of Stornoway Castle, the Macleod stronghold, but rubble beneath Stornoway's quays (the present Lews Castle was built in Victorian times). But there is a rocky fortress, the island of Berisay, to remind us of the Macleod Barons who, whatever their faults, never gave in to Lowland threats and, in ousting the Fife Adventurers, kept Lewis singularly Highland — and safe from the divisiveness which has been the fate of other planted communities.

8.

THE MACKENZIE EARLS OF SEAFORTH

COLIN MACKENZIE, *1st Earl of Seaforth (d. 1633)*

The Mackenzies were in control but they were wary of the Macleods, who could be expected to seek vengeance for their downfall. There was nothing to fear across the Minch, where the family held power; but in Uig there lived many Macleods, with their Macdonald allies, and they were also numerous in the Stornoway area.

And so the Mackenzies built a round tower, commanding a magnificent view to west and east, at the head of Loch Seaforth. Maclennans, Macraes and Macivers — clans friendly to the Mackenzies — were placed in key positions in Carloway, overlooking Uig, and also in the Lochs area between the tower and Stornoway.

Colin Mackenzie was married to Lady Margaret Seton. He had no male heirs, so that the title passed to his brother George.

STORNOWAY'S SHORT-LIVED ROYAL CHARTER

In order to promote local trade, Colin Mackenzie secured a Charter from King Charles I which made Stornoway a royal burgh. The royal burghs had the monopoly of foreign trade, with rights of export of Lewis commodities and full rights of all loch fishing in Lewis. Stornoway had rich fisheries, beef, tallow (for making candles), wool and woven goods for export. But the other Scottish royal burghs refused to accept Stornoway into their ranks; instead, they petitioned the King, with great determination, for the removal of Stornoway's royal burgh status. They argued that Dutchmen brought to Lewis by Seaforth to help organise local trade might instead promote Dutch fishing interests in the area, to the detriment of Britain. And so the grant of the Charter was revoked. The move was unjust, and limiting to the growth of island trade and prosperity.

GEORGE MACKENZIE, *2nd Earl of Seaforth (d. 1651)*

The distinctive way of life and language of the clans had long set them apart from the people of the Lowlands. Mountains, long arms of the sea and lack of roads had isolated them, so that they had been little concerned with anything outside their own communities. But in the 17th and 18th centuries the clans began to play a larger part in the affairs of Scotland as a whole, and even of England.

Involvement came in the Civil War, which began in 1642. At first George Mackenzie fought against the Royalists in 1645 at the Battle of Auldearn, where only three of the 300-strong Lewis contingent survived, but later he went over to the King. George Mackenzie was married to Lady Barbara Forbes, and they had a large family.

KENNETH MACKENZIE, *3rd Earl of Seaforth (d. 1678)*

Kenneth Mackenzie, who was married to Isobel Mackenzie of Tarbat, was a staunch Royalist, and he was on the side of the King when the Royalists were finally defeated at Worcester in 1651, with immense loss of life among the Highland clans, especially the Macleods of Harris. Later, Kenneth Mackenzie rashly captured the crew of one of Oliver Cromwell's ships and Cromwell sent troops to garrison Stornoway. Although several soldiers were killed in an affray with the Mackenzies, Cromwell's men held the garrison. They then battered down the old Stornoway Castle and built a fort to guard the harbour from the Dutch, with whom the country was at war.

Perhaps the strict religious exercises of the Puritan soldiers were admired by the people of Lewis. They were certainly remembered by the Presbyterian Fathers who, centuries later, re-named the main street of Stornoway Cromwell Street after the conqueror who came to be regarded as a hero.

KENNETH MACKENZIE, *4th Earl of Seaforth (d. 1701)*

Many would say that it was their adherence to the Jacobite cause which drained the resources of the Seaforths and ultimately caused their downfall. In 1688 the Roman Catholic King, James VII and II, was ousted in a bloodless revolution. Those who continued to support him were known as Jacobites, from *Jacobus,* the Latin word for James.

Kenneth Mackenzie was a Jacobite; he followed James into exile and was awarded the title of Baron Fortrose. He later returned to Scotland to join the Jacobite struggle there, and was captured and imprisoned for over six years. He was married to Lady Frances Herbert, and they had one son and one daughter.

WILLIAM MACKENZIE, *5th Earl of Seaforth (d. 1740)*

William Mackenzie followed the Jacobite tradition. Much of his youth had been spent in France, and in 1708 he was imprisoned on suspicion of being involved in an attempted invasion of Scotland by France in the Jacobite cause. In 1715 he fought at the head of 3,000 men at the Battle of Sheriffmuir, and, because of this, all his estates and honours were forfeited. But he escaped to Lewis, and then to France, the Jacobite refuge.

In 1719 he was again involved in a Jacobite rising, all the planning for which was carried out at Seaforth Lodge, the family's Stornoway residence (built on the site of the present day Lews Castle at the end of the 17th century but demolished in the middle of the 19th century). Spanish ships, Spanish troops, muskets and ammunition were acquired, but the rising was defeated at Glenshiel, and William Mackenzie was again forced to flee to France. About 1725, however, he was freed of the threat of execution or imprisonment. He bought back the estates and returned to Lewis. His wife was Mary Kenet of Northumberland and they had four children.

In 1954 a small earthenware container with a hoard of coins was unearthed near the site of the Seaforth Lodge. The hoard consisted of Scottish, English, Irish, Netherlands and Swedish coins, the latest date being 1669. Perhaps a soldier in one of the early Jacobite risings decided to safeguard his money before he set out; if so, it seems that he never returned.

KENNETH MACKENZIE, *who adopted the title Baron Fortrose because of his father's attainder (d.1761)*

With the family's misfortunes in the Jacobite cause, it is hardly surprising that Kenneth Mackenzie, son of the attainted Earl William, decided against coming out for Charles Edward Stewart — Bonnie Prince Charlie— in the Rising of 1745. After the defeat of the Prince's cause at Culloden he was hunted in the Highlands, and he eventually reached Lewis; but the people did not betray him, even for the reward of £30,000, and he found food and shelter with the Roman Catholic Laird of Kildun. A cairn on Arnish moor marks the spot where the Prince spent a night before escaping, after many adventures, from the nine warships patrolling the Minch searching for him, and being taken aboard a ship for France and safety.

Lord Fortrose's wife was Lady Mary Stewart of Galloway. They had six daughters and a son.

KENNETH MACKENZIE, *created Earl of Seaforth in 1771 (d. 1781)*

Some thirty years after the last Jacobite rising of 1745 the fortune of the Seaforths was completely gone. The properties never recovered from the vast sums spent in the Stewart cause. In serious financial difficulties, the Earl sold the estates to his cousin, Thomas Mackenzie, for £100,000. Kenneth Mackenzie raised the Seaforth Highlanders regiment, and was Lieutenant-Colonel in command. He died, aged 37, on passage to India with the regiment. His wife Lady Caroline Stanhope died aged 20 in 1767. They had one daughter.

THOMAS MACKENZIE, *afterwards* **MACKENZIE-HUMBERSTON** *(d. 1783)*

Thomas Mackenzie was a distinguished soldier, and he assumed command of the Seaforth Highlanders on the death of the Earl of Seaforth. Humberston was his mother's family name. He was unmarried and did not long survive the cousin from whom he had bought the estates, for he died of cannon-shot wounds received in a sea battle in India in 1783.

FRANCIS HUMBERSTON MACKENZIE, *created Lord Seaforth, Baron Mackenzie of Kintail in 1797 (d. 1815)*

> I see into the far future and I read the doom of the race of my oppressor. The long descended line of Seaforth will, ere many generations have passed, end in extinction and sorrow.

I see a Chief, the last of his House, both deaf and dumb. He will be father of four fair sons, all of whom he will follow to the tomb. He will live careworn and die mourning, knowing that the honours of his House are to be extinguished for ever and that no future Chief of the Mackenzies shall bear rule in Kintail.

After lamenting over the last and most promising of his sons, he himself shall sink into the grave and the remnant of his possessions shall be inherited by a white-coifed lassie from the east; and she is to kill her sister. [10.]

These are the words of "The Doom of Kintail", alleged to be one of the prophecies of Coinneach Odhar, Kenneth Mackenzie, the Lewis seer about whom there are many stories. And they do describe what happened in the life of Francis Humberston Mackenzie. As a boy the Earl had contracted scarlet fever, which left him deaf. He and his wife, Mary Proby of Litchfield, had a large family of six daughters and four sons, but all his sons died before him. When the last of his sons died the Earl was struck dumb with shock, and he died the following year. His elder daughter Mary, recently widowed, returned home wearing the white coif (head-dress) of mourning usual in the West Indies, where she had been living. Later she took one of her sisters for a ride in a pony carriage and the ponies bolted, throwing out the sisters, the younger of whom was killed. Mary was by that time married to James Stewart of Glasserton who added the name Mackenzie to his own.

In 1844, again widowed, Mary Stewart Mackenzie, sold Lewis to James (later Sir James) Matheson of Sutherland, who had gained a fortune in the Far East. Her grandson, James Stewart Mackenzie, was created Baron Seaforth in 1921; but he died two years later without male heirs, and the title again became extinct. The Kintail Estate was later given over to the National Trust.

The Seaforths were adventurous men, and for this they paid a high price. They neglected their people for the Jacobite cause and drained all the resources of the estates. In an attempt to increase his dwindling fortune, the last of the Lewis Seaforths evicted many people in order to introduce new sheep farms, beginning the fashion for large farms which was the cause of great hardship for the people, as we shall see.

They took the name of the sea loch in east Lewis — Loch Seaforth — and made it a famous, military name, so that this longest of all the sea lochs of Lewis must continually remind us of the Mackenzie clan chiefs and their influence on the island over two centuries.

DUN CARLOWAY FROM AN ENGRAVING C. 1875

STORNOWAY HARBOUR FROM THE GALLOWS HILL, C. 1875

9.

LATER LITERATURE AND MUSIC

We have already seen (in translation) some examples of the early Gaelic poetry, most of which comes to us from Ireland. For many centuries there was a common classical Gaelic used for poetry in Ireland and Scotland and examples of poems composed in this literary language can be found in the famous book which was compiled by the Dean of Lismore, Sir James Macgregor, early in the 16th century. This is the oldest collection of Gaelic poetry to have survived in Scotland. The most distinguished line of classical bards in Scotland was the MacMhuirich family, who became bards to Clan Donald and who wrote most of the collection of history and lore known as the Books of Clanranald. Eventually, however, the classical language gave way as a medium to the natural Gaelic of the people, and compositions in that form can readily be understood by Gaelic speakers of the present day.

A considerable body of songs and poems survives from the period of the sixteenth and seventeenth century. Many are praise poems to chiefs, genealogies or satires; but there are others on the universal themes of love and war, and others on religion, hunting etc. There are laments and lullabies, and work songs to accompany activities such as rowing, reaping and, in particular, the waulking (shrinking and rolling) of tweed, so that poetry and song was clearly closely connected with everyday activities of people.

Each clan had its bard or singer, its harpist and its piper. The early bards had followed a strict code of training; they were succeeded by poets without the formal training, but still attached to particular clans. Two of the most outstanding were Màiri Nighean Alasdair Ruaidh (Mary Macleod) of Harris and Dunvegan and Iain Lom (John Macdonald), who was related to the Macdonalds of Keppoch. Closely involved with the Earls of Seaforth were the poets Alasdair Mackenzie of Achilty and his son Murdo (Murchadh Mòr), who both acted as their Chamberlain in Lewis, and Murdo Matheson, Bard of Seaforth. In Mull, the poet Eachann Bacach (Hector the Lame) was related to the Macleans of Duart.

But the old ways were changing and the outside world encroaching, with its different ways, ways which the chiefs sometimes adopted, so that their life-style was not always as that of their ancestors had been, and as the bards would have wished. Born in Bragar, Lewis, Roderick Morison, *An Clàrsair Dall* (The Blind Harpist), was also a fine bard, and in this translation of a verse from his poem to Macleod of Dunvegan he criticises these changes.

> Echo is dejected in the hall where music was wont to sound, in the place resorted to by poet-bands, now without mirth, or pleasure, or drinking, without merriment or entertainment, without the passing round of drinking-horns

in close succession, without feeling, without feasting, without liberality to men of learning, without dalliance, or voice raised in tuneful song. [11.]

THE LAMONT HARP, OF WEST HIGHLAND WORKMANSHIP, C. 1500

The harpists were largely silenced by the rise of the bagpipes to favour, the growing popularity of the fiddle and the difficulty of learning to play the harp. Just as the harp had followed the lyre, the bagpipes began to rival the harp in the 16th century, with their music of salute and lament, the pibroch (known in Gaelic as *Ceòl Mòr*, "the Great Music," *Ceòl Beag* being the lighter music such as reels and jigs).

The playing of pibroch replaced the custom of keening (from the Gaelic word *caoine* which appears, although with a modified meaning, in modern Scottich Gaelic as caoineadh), when women had walked before a funeral procession, repeating certain rhymes and clapping hands to keep time; and it also took over from the coronach, or elegy for the dead. Not at first favoured in Lewis, piping became popular, with some very fine modern pipers, such as Pipe-Major Donald Macleod of Stornoway and Pipe-Major Ian Morrison of Back.

The fiddle, introduced in the 17th century, was regarded with jealousy by the piper. It has long been associated with merriment and dance, and it introduced the Strathspey in addition to the faster music of the reels and jigs.

The 18th century Highlands produced several exceptional Gaelic poets — Alexander Macdonald (Alasdair Mac Mhaighstir Alasdair), John MacCodrum, Rob Donn Mackay, William Ross, Dugald Buchanan and Duncan Ban Macintyre. *Donnchadh Bàn nan Oran* — Fair-haired Duncan of the Songs — is particularly noted for his vivid poems about nature. This is from a translation by Iain Crichton Smith of one of his most famous, "Moladh Beinn Dòbhrain" (Praise of Ben Dorain), in which the poet describes the majesty of the great mountain and reveals his love of the deer to be found on it.

> The hind that's sharp-headed
> is fierce in its speeding:
> how delicate, rapid
> its nostrils, wind-reading!
> Light-hooved and quick limbèd,
> she runs on the summit;
> from that uppermost limit
> no gun will remove her.
> You'll not see her winded,
> that elegant mover.
>
> Her forebears were healthy.
> When she stopped to take breath then,
> how I love the pure wraith-like
> sound of her calling ... [12.]

Eighteenth-century Gaelic poetry shows great variety, and whether the theme is love, the beauty of the natural world, Jacobitism or the spiritual life, there is a tremendous richness of vocabulary and an exhuberant, almost rapturous, use of language.

In 1762, after anonymously publishing *Fragments of Ancient Poetry* ...., James Macpherson published *Fingal*, an epic in six books, and it was followed by *Temora* and other poems. These were represented as the genuine works of the poet Ossian, composed in the 3rd century AD and now taken from ancient Gaelic manuscripts. They created a great deal of controversy, for their origins seemed extremely obscure, and a search began for genuine ancient literature which might exist in the Highlands, either orally or in manuscript. It eventually became clear that such did exist, although only in a limited number of cases does a Gaelic ballad correspond closely to Macpherson's 'translations'.

The efforts of private collectors, the re-discovery of the Book of the Dean of Lismore — compiled early in the sixteenth century but containing poetry already hundreds of years old when it was written down there — and the work of the Highland Society, formed in Edinburgh in 1784, were important in establishing how much of the older poetry had survived. Ironically, however, it was the work of Macpherson that awoke the romantic interest of other countries in Europe in Gaelic literature and in the Highlands generally — an interest that persists to this day.

In the early 19th century John Morrison was writing his *Traditions of the Western Isles*. Born in Harris in 1787, he moved as a boy to Uig, where he later became a teacher, before taking up the trade of cooper in Stornoway. Many of his stories are based on history; others are legends about the Fèinn.

However, the 19th century also saw the religious revival which silenced, in the name of Calvinism, the poem, the song, the dance and the music of the fiddle. A melancholy silence fell over a Lewis also oppressed by poverty.

In the 1860s there was a renewal of interest in the ancient works, and the collections of John Francis Campbell of Islay (Iain Og Ile) proved that as well as the old poems and songs there was a Gaelic literature of prose tales and legends, many relating to the Fèinn, which had been familiar to the people over many centuries.

Alexander Carmichael, an Excise Officer, wrote down many Gaelic hymns and incantations relating to ancient rites in the Highlands and Islands from oral recitation, and these were later published (some of them after his death) in his famous collection *Carmina Gadelica*. The Dewar Manuscripts of oral traditions were collected in Argyll, and the Gaelic Societies of Inverness (founded in 1871) and Glasgow (founded in 1887) continued this work of rescue and preservation, as well as promoting everything Gaelic and Highland. Unfortunately, the fashion for teaching all things English saw to it that not enough of this reached the people, and particularly the children in the new schools affected by the 1872 Education Act. Much of the old tradition was in danger of being forgotten.

But by the 1870s in Lewis the melancholy mood was gone. Bards spoke out against Clearance and injustice, and a new mood in Gaelic literature appears in the uncompromising verse of John Smith, Malcolm Mackay and Donald Macdonald.

WHITE SANDS OF THE BAY OF UIG, C. 1875

There is open pride in this translation of part of Murdo Macleod's famous song 'Eilean an Fhraoich' (Isle of the Heather):

O Isle of the heather, my heart longs for thee,
Like the salmon, the plover, the deer to be free;
Where by loch, sound and river, in green strath and glen,
Thrive the choicest of cattle, the bravest of men.

Our little grey Lews has for all time stood forth
The gem of the ocean, the pride of the north;
May the sun's guiding glory upon her be shed,
That her crops may have increase, her people be fed. [13.]

It should, however, be noted that the collections and societies of the 19th century were often initiated by the well-to-do. A romantic picture of Highland life had begun to become popular, and this was encouraged by Sir Walter Scott's depiction of Highland history and scenery in his novels and poems, by the growth of the tartan industry and by the adoption of Balmoral as a home by Queen Victoria and Prince Albert. The way in which Gaelic music was presented often reflected the genteel tastes of the time — so that, for example, traditional Gaelic songs might be arranged for piano accompaniment in Edinburgh drawing-rooms in a way which diluted their quality and did them scant justice.

An Comunn Gaidhealach (The Highland Society) was founded in 1891, and its yearly Mods (Gaelic festivals) promote the use of the language and its literature and music. The number of Lewis winners of the Bardic Crown or medals for singing, including the greatly prized Gold medals, is too great to list.

THE MODERN WRITERS

In the Highlands, bards have continued to compose in the Gaelic language. Comparatively recent Lewis bards have included Murdo Macfarlane of Melbost, who wrote poetry and popular songs. His work, and that of other bards, especially Angus Campbell of Ness, who has written poetry and a fascinating Gaelic autobigraphy, has become well known, even outside the island.

But while the traditional type of Gaelic poetry has continued to be composed by the 'local' bards, another style has become firmly established as well. Some trace the beginnings of this style, a style more like modern poetry in other countries, in the work of John Munro (killed in the First World War), Murdo Murray and James Thomson, and it has undergone further development in the work of the five leading modern Gaelic poets— Sorley Maclean of Raasay (1911-96), George Campbell Hay of Kintyre (1915-84) and three Lewismen, Derick Thomson (born in 1921), Iain Crichton Smith (1928-98), who was also a renowned novelist, and Donald MacAulay (born in 1930). Donald MacAulay is the editor of the anthology *Nua-Bhàrdachd Ghàidhlig* (English title *Modern Scottish Gaelic Poems*), which contains a selection of the work of all five, with translations.

Here is a translation of a Gaelic poem by Iain Crichton Smith, 'Tha Thu air Aigeann M'inntinn' (You are at the Bottom of My Mind):

Without my knowing it you are at the bottom of my mind,
like one who visits the bottom of the sea with his helmet
and his two great eyes; and I do not know properly your
expression or your manner after five years of the showers
of time pouring between you and me.

Nameless mountains of water pouring between me, hauling
you on board, and your expression and manners in my
weak hands. You went astray among the mysterious foliage
of the sea-bottom in the green half-light without love.

And you'll never rise to the surface of the sea, even though
my hands should be ceaselessly hauling, and I do not know
your way at all, you in the half-light of your sleep, haunting
the bottom of the sea without ceasing, and I hauling on the
surface of the ocean. [14.]

And this is Donald MacAulay's translation of his own poem 'Do Charaid' (For a Friend):

A change has come upon your face that was like the
sunshine; in the midst of your aspiring strength you
received the thorn crown and knew the taste of blood on
your tongue: the sod is cut from beneath your feet.

It is sad for me, that today your back is towards a berry-red
sun in the grey trees, that you are losing the power to hear
the crackle of the frost underfoot, are moving into stillness and silence.

The words come crushed from my lips speckling the page;
Guaire lives not nor Cuchuilin; O young warrior for whom
are shed my tears, my mouth is not poetic. [15.]

Although the Lewis writers have often gone to live on the mainland, their work shows that they feel themselves part of these islands wherever they may be; and they give of their wider experience in a strange and beautiful blend of realism and nostalgia, as shown in this translation of a Gaelic poem by Ruaraidh MacThòmais (Derick Thomson), *Bùrn is Mòine 's Coirc* (Water and Peats and Oats):

"Water and peats and oats" —
a word in a stranger's mouth,
in the throng of the town,
in the town of the strangers.
Madness! The foolish heart
lapping along these ancient rocks
as though there were no sea-journey in the world
but that one.
The heart tied to a tethering post, round upon round of
the rope
till it grows short,
and the mind free.
I bought its freedom dearly. [16.]

Later Lewis writers of note include Norman Campbell, Norman Malcolm Macdonald, Donald Maclean, Finlay Macleod, John Murray and poets Anna Frater, Siùsaidh Nicnèill and Ian Stephen. The literature thus preserves for us a very fine picture of the present and of the past.

10.

THE PRESBYTERIAN CHURCH

A decline in the moral standards of the clergy led to 16th century Scotland being increasingly influenced by the ideas of the Reformation. A period of strife followed between the Reformers and the Crown, which favoured retaining the old Roman Catholic faith.

When the Protestant Church was established, disputes continued over the form the new Church should take. Some wished for a Presbyterian system with a Church ruled by kirk sessions, presbyteries and a general assembly, while others wanted an Episcopalian system with bishops and archbishops.

Presbyterianism gained the upper hand in Scotland, but the Episcopalian system was favoured in England. Argument over this led in 1638 to the National Covenant, pledging support to Presbyterianism in Scotland, and then to civil war when King Charles I attempted to impose the Anglican system. It was not until 1690, after the Roman Catholic King James VII and II was deposed, that the Scottish Church finally became officially Presbyterian.

In the Hebrides, after the Reformation, most of the Church lands were seized by the Chiefs. At first an Episcopalian system was favoured, but later they supported the National Covenant in the hopes of protecting their property. During the Civil War the people supported the line of the chiefs out of duty, not because of personal religious fervour. Because of all these changes, little ill-feeling developed between the different creeds, although some strife continued between Roman Catholics and Protestants. The Seaforths, being Roman Catholic and in a position of power, were treated with suspicion by the 17th century Presbyterian ministers, who carried large swords and guarded their churches with armed men.

Throughout the 18th and 19th centuries, several quarrels within the Church of Scotland led to splinter groups leaving to set up separate Presbyterian Churches. In the 1830s dissent arose over the nomination of ministers, which was, in effect, carried out by landowners, not by the ordinary people. When Parliament paid no attention to a petition denouncing this, hundreds of ministers walked out and, in 1843 founded the Free Church of Scotland.

Lewis has some of the largest Free Church congregations in Scotland. Though more austere in outlook than the Church of Scotland (the original Presbyterian Church), it is less strict than the Free Presbyterian Church, founded in 1893 by those who thought the theology of the Free Church too liberal.

Episcopal Churches are those of St Molua at Europie and St Peter's in Stornoway; in the latter there is a famous Prayer Book which belonged to David Livingstone. There is a Roman Catholic Church in Stornoway, and there are also groups of other religious persuasions.

The Christian faith has been staunchly held by the people of Lewis over many centuries, often intermingling with Celtic pagan beliefs, but clinging on through religious upheavals and domestic strife to emerge in the rather severe Calvinistic form of the 19th and 20th centuries. Despite modern influences, change and doubt, the long-held beliefs cannot fade easily.

THE GAELIC LANGUAGE

The Gaelic language of the first Scots was also the language of many of the Celtic Christian missionaries and of the early Scots kings and their subjects. But outside influences steadily encroached upon it. Anglo-Saxon and Norman culture, introduced at the royal court, spread in the Lowlands, so that by the 13th century Inglis, as it was known, was spoken in many areas south of the Highland line. But Gaelic continued to flourish among the northern clans, and there was the great flowering of Gaelic poetry in the 17th and 18th centuries.

Eventually, southern influences reached north beyond the Highland line; and after the Jacobite Rising of 1745 attempts were made to stamp out Gaelic altogether. Children were beaten for speaking Gaelic in school or playground, or the oppressive Maide Gàidhlig ('Gaelic Stick'), a leather loop with a baton attached, was strung round their necks to punish them and to remind them that Gaelic was no longer to be spoken. By imposing English upon the Gaelic-speaking Highlanders in this way, the Government thought to bring them more under control. Before long, English-speaking incomers filled many important posts. English, it seemed, spelled success, and was made to appear more desirable than Gaelic.

Because of their remoteness, and because organised education in English was later in arriving, Lewis and the other Hebridean islands held on to the Gaelic language when it was lost in other parts of the Highlands. Immense emigrations, some caused by the eviction of people from the land, further greatly depleted the Gaelic-speaking population, although some Gaelic-speaking communities organised themselves abroad — especially in Canada, where there are still speakers of Gaelic descended from settlers from the Highlands.

But Lewis, although it kept the language, suffered like other places from the elevation of English over Gaelic in educational and commercial spheres — in which, in effect, a subtle sense of inferiority was associated with the speaking of Gaelic until very recently. But at the present time there is clear evidence of a re-discovery of identity in the Gaelic-speaking areas, including Lewis, and pride in their own heritage is shown by the formation of many societies, such as Comunn Eachdraidh Nis (Ness), who are responsible for local historical surveys. And Gaelic is being used more widely than ever in early education, particularly in the Western Isles, where the Bilingual Education Project was set up in 1975.

But the survival of Gaelic in Lewis, as elsewhere, against so many odds, is chiefly owed to the parents who continued to speak it to their children in the home. And that is still the greatest hope for the language. Despite all the difficulties, if the people insist strongly enough that their own language must at all costs be safeguarded, it surely will be.

Gaelic has long been a language of literature, and we have already seen (in translation) some of the works. But literature in modern Gaelic, and the poetry in particular, is also of such quality that it can take an honourable place among other literatures of the present day — a very great achievement, when we consider the difficulties which the language has had to face. We owe a particular debt to the modern Gaelic writers, who have not only preserved the literary tradition but also developed it and adapted it to the needs of the present.

As we have seen, one of the leading modern poets was Somhairle MacGill-Eain (Sorley MacLean) of Raasay. Here is one of his many beautiful love-poems, followed by his own translation:

REOTHAIRT

Uair is uair agus mi briste
thig mo smuain ort is tu òg,
is lìonaidh an cuan do-thuigsinn
le làn-mara 's mìle seòl.

Falaichear cladach na trioblaid
le bhodhannan is tiùrr a' bhròin
is buailidh an tonn gun bhristeadh
mu m' chasan le suathadh sròil.

Ciamar nach do mhair an reothairt
bu bhuidhe dhomh na do na h-eòin
agus a chaill mi a cobhair
's i tràghadh boinn' air bhoinne bròin?

SPRING TIDE

Again and again when I am broken
my thought comes on you when you were young,
and the incomprehensible ocean fills
with floodtide and a thousand sails.

The shore of trouble is hidden
with its reefs and the wrack of grief,
and the unbreaking wave strikes
about my feet with a silken rubbing.

How did the spring tide not last,
the spring tide more golden to me than to the birds,
and how did I lose its succour,
ebbing drop by drop of grief? [17.]

11.

THE END OF THE CLAN SYSTEM

After the defeat at Culloden, the Jacobite Highlanders on the field were treated with great severity. The wounded were stabbed with bayonets or shot. Those taken prisoner were shipped to England for trial and were either executed or were imprisoned under terrible conditions, so that many died or suffered broken health. Others were transported to the plantations of North America, and few of these ever saw their homes again. Throughout the Highlands, fugitives were hunted and shot, while the houses of Jacobite sympathisers were burned down and their cattle driven off.

Acts were passed removing the legal powers of the chiefs, forbidding the carrying of arms, the use of Highland dress — the tartan plaid and kilt — and the bagpipes were condemned (being considered instruments of war). Speaking the Gaelic language in public and school was discouraged.

These actions destroyed much of the Highland way of life and weakened the ties between the chiefs and their people. Usurped of their authority, many chiefs moved to Edinburgh and London, running up debts in the upkeep of mansions and in high living. The tacksmen were left in virtual control, and they ousted many sub-tenants to make way for black cattle, for beef was in great demand in England. The chiefs, in their turn, demanded exorbitant rents from the tacksmen; but in the 1760s harvests failed and cattle died, and later prices fell, but not rents, so that many tacksmen emigrated.

Factors were then appointed by the chiefs to raise as much money as possible from their Highland estates. Unlike the tacksmen, they generally had no longstanding local links or bonds of kinship. The split was complete. In Lewis, where many of the Seaforths had already long been absentee landlords, matters could hardly have been worse. In other areas rents soon doubled and trebled. The only outlet for those who could not pay was emigration, but being destitute, they were forced to offer themselves as servants and labourers to be exported to North American estates.

This led to fraudulent contracts and kidnapping, for money was to be made from the sale of servants abroad. In 1774 several ships were sailing in Hebridean waters taking people aboard under false promises or kidnapping them. One of these, the *Philadelphia*, was reported to have kidnapped boys off the beach at Stornoway. These ships were small and often unseaworthy, and many of those on board died of disease on the voyage.

For those who remained there was the new threat of eviction to make room for sheep. The demand for British wool and mutton greatly increased when the American War of Independence (1775-1783) and the Napoleonic Wars (1793-1815) dried up North American and French sources of supply. It was discovered that the Cheviot breed could stand up to cold winters — in fact, flourished in the Highlands

— and needed little tending. Now people became a nuisance; all the land was required for sheep.

And so the people were removed to the rocky, infertile areas, to poor, undrained land, the very edge of the seashore, to other overcrowded villages, or were forced to emigrate, while the good land and pasture was given over to sheep and deer. Eventually the Highlands were to become severely depopulated.

CROFTING

But the tenants in the overcrowded villages became less able to support themselves. The houses, at first grouped together on the arable land (using a system of run-rig — plots for agriculture changing hands every three years or so), began to spread out in a new allocation in order to divide what was left. Finally, in Lewis, long thin strips, each with a share of good and poor land, came into being, with the houses strung out along the tracks that were becoming roads. This system of one tenant to one holding is known as crofting.

High rents were charged, regardless of the quality of the land, and many people had turned to kelp-making and illegal whisky distilling to avoid eviction. Kelp, the alkaline ash of seaweed, was used in the manufacture of soap, linen and glass. Kelp-making was not on such a large scale in Lewis as, for example, in the Uists; but Loch Roag kelp was of very high quality and commanded a good price, and kelp-making was also important in the fiords of the Lochs area.

The boom in kelp spread a false sense of security in the islands, and the population rose greatly. But after the Napoleonic Wars ended in 1815, other sources of the material became available and the Hebridean trade slumped. Economic chaos followed, and thousands of islanders were left destitute. The slump hit rich and poor; some chiefs, such as Macleod of Harris and Dunvegan, were ruined attempting to aid their people to emigrate or buy relief produce. And before very long all the Outer Isles were to be sold.

THE CLEARANCES

Evictions intensified. In Sutherland the roofs were burned over the people's head to hurry them out, and in Harris the people were moved by the new owner to the rocky east coast, where there was hardly enough soil to bury the dead and plots for agriculture consisted of peat and seaweed built up in hollows.

In Lewis, areas such as Uig, which contained good pasture for sheep, were being cleared, with the evicted families moving to the remaining areas and causing great congestion. By the 1850s the population of Uig, now 60% greater than in 1800, was crowded into about half the area. Use of the hill grazing left to them was severely restricted to certain days only, with strict penalties if they were found there at any other time.

The other areas worst affected were Park, and the north of Stornoway parish. In Park over twenty villages were cleared and the people moved to other already overcrowded areas or forced to emigrate. This was the policy of the last of the Lewis Seaforths, who introduced and let out sheep farms in order to alleviate his economic difficulties. The policy was continued during the time of his daughter Mary and her husband James Stewart-Mackenzie, and of Sir James Matheson, so that there were more than twenty such farms eventually, most of them run by incomers from the mainland. Four large areas were also set aside for deer.

Many other parts of Lewis escaped only because they were found unsuitable for sheep farms. Much of the area of East Loch Roag and Carloway kept its crofts, a famous exception being the old village of Dalmore, which was cleared for sheep and lies ghost-like to this day:

Round the hearth that warmed the children grows the nettle,
And the thistle blocks the doorway as I pass;
Where was once the garden patch, the rabbits settle,
And the road is thickly carpeted by grass.

In the far-off graves, in exile, rest the ashes
Of the men whose hearts were ever buried here;
And their children say, "This wild Atlantic dashes
Yonder, eastwards, on a coast that is more dear.

Though our eyes have never seen, and ne'er may see it,
Yet a whisper in our hearts still names it home;
And a strange voice calls, howe'er we flee it,
Saying, softly, like a ghostly mother, 'Come'." [18.]

But why the people accepted such treatment is the much asked question. The reasons are not hard to find: the people were far from the centre of Government, spoke a different language, formal education was limited and they had no voting rights until the end of the 19th century. And their only leaders, the clergy (themselves economically dependent on the landlords), advised resigned acceptance, with escape to religion the only answer. But if for a time there was the appearance of acceptance, in spirit the people were a proud people, and in the end they rebelled.

The people lived mainly on fish and potatoes, so that the potato blights which occurred in the 1840s left them extremely vulnerable. Famine was widespread but, of necessity, they found a way out in the seasonal migrations to the fishing in Caithness and other east coast areas of Scotland and England. These were to support the island people for over 70 years. But it was too late for the thousands from northern Scotland which the Highlands and Islands Emigration Society (formed in 1851) assisted to go abroad, mainly to Australia. These included some from Lewis and

St Kilda. Many more Lewis people had no choice but to accept subsidised passages to Canada, in the 1850s, which were provided by Sir James Matheson, advocate of emigration during the years of poverty which followed the potato famine.

THE FISHING INDUSTRY

At first the fishing was mainly in the summer, which fitted in with seed-time and harvest on the croft. Later it expanded greatly. Men and women were both involved, the men working the boats, the women gutting and packing. It was harsh, hard work, under the most difficult conditions. It is referred to in the poem 'Do Mo Mhàthair' (To My Mother) by Iain Mac a' Ghobhainn (Iain Crichton Smith). His mother was one of those who travelled the coasts and gutted the herring by hand, in a tradition which continued until the 1930s, when machines came into use:

You were gutting herring in distant Yarmouth, and the salt
sun in the morning rising out of the sea, the blood on the
edge of your knife, and that salt so coarse that it stopped
you from speaking and made your lips bitter.

I was in Aberdeen sucking new courses, my Gaelic in a
book and my Latin at the tiller, sitting there on a chair with
my coffee beside me and leaves shaking the sails of
scholarship and my intelligence.

Guilt is tormenting me because of what happened and how
things are. I would not like to be getting up in the darkness
of the day gutting and tearing the fish of the morning on
the shore and that savage sea to be roaring down my gloves
without cease.

Though I do that in my poetry, it is my own blood that is
on my hands, and every herring that the high tide gave me
palpitating till I make a song, and instead of a cooper my
language always hard and strict on me, and the coarse salt
on my ring bringing animation to death. [19.]

Fishing locally with lines from boats for white fish, such as cod and ling, long remained very important, and as well as providing fresh food, fish were dried and salted for winter use or for sale.

LAND AGITATION

But the fishing was not always dependable, with periods of decline, especially in the 1880s. Once again facing poverty, hardened fisherfolk and a new generation which questioned and did not accept the unfair system took a much more militant line. Agitation for the land began, for enlarged holdings meant less congestion and greater food production. The crofters demanded the return of the land which had been taken in the Clearances. But, when this was not forthcoming, they withheld rent, banded together to take land from the landlords and the sheep farmers, and stood out in defiance of attempts to evict them for their actions.

The Highlander, a newspaper set up in Inverness in 1873 by John Murdoch, an Islayman, became the chief mouthpiece of the crofters, preaching that the land was the people's and demanding Highland Land Law reform — security of tenure, fair rents and more land, to ease poverty and put an end to injustice.

Agitation became widespread in the Highlands and Islands in the 1880s, but it made itself felt in Lewis as early as 1874, when the crofters of Bernera resisted by a show of force an attempt to evict over fifty of their number. They then marched on Lews Castle, Stornoway, where the proprietor, Sir James Matheson, claimed to be unaware of the policy of hounding and harrassment prosecuted by his Chamberlain over many years. The people of Bernera kept their land, but it was later stated that Sir James Matheson had an estate policy

... of territorial aggrandisement and despotic power, so absolute and arbitrary as to be almost universally complained of. [20.]

After the Bernera Riot, the proprietor made some concessions. Agricultural prices were falling in any case, and tenants for the estates were becoming harder to find. But it was not enough. In 1881 in Ireland, where a similar struggle was taking place, a fair land settlement was granted, and this encouraged the Highland crofters to fight for the same concession. In 1882 in Braes, Skye, crofters threatened with eviction confronted police in a pitched battle. In 1883 in Lewis, several hundred crofters from Uig and many from other areas demonstrated in Stornoway, to demand the restoration of the land.

The Highland Land Law Reform Association (The Land League) was set up, and crofters began to join in large numbers, holding huge demonstrations in support of the cause. Help came from expatriate Highlanders in British cities who held meetings on behalf of the crofters and collected funds to pay any legal expenses incurred by the agitation. The crofters' plight gained publicity throughout Britain. But the granting of the vote to crofters in 1884 was the greatest single factor in their favour, enabling them for the first time to elect MPs sympathetic to their cause.

The Free Church was based on opposition to the landlords and symbolised a new feeling of pride among its people. But few ministers of religion spoke out in favour of crofter action, with notable exceptions, however, including the Rev. Donald

MacCallum, for a time Church of Scotland minister in Lochs, Lewis, and the Rev. Evan Gordon, Free Church minister in Glasgow.

THE NAPIER COMMISSION

As agitation spread to Barra, the Uists, Tiree and many other areas, Parliament took action and in 1883 appointed a Royal Commission, under Lord Francis Napier, to go round various villages in the Highlands and Islands collecting facts, in order to work out ways of improving conditions and restoring order.

It was a sorry tale. Napier Campbell, a solicitor in Stornoway, listed the people's grievances:

1. Wholesale evictions from good land now under sheep and deer, for example, Morsgail, Lynshader and Park.

2. Shifting whole townships and sometimes individuals from place to place without any compensation for improvements.

3. Individual evictions of a revengeful or capricious nature.

4. Encroachments and readjustments to their loss ... families increase, holdings diminish. The rent remains the same.

5. The arable land, and sometimes the grazing, limited and very poor.

6. Rents in excess of the true agricultural and pastoral value of the land.

7. Verbal lease for one year, terminable at Whitsunday, engendering a condition of servility, listlessness and dependence.

8. Virtually no law for their redress. [21.]

Neil Maclennan, a crofter at Breasclete, gave an example from his own experience in one of the many items of information collected by the Commission.

"We were formerly in Reef, where we were born and brought up, as also our fathers and grandfathers. The land there was good, and was quite convenient to the sea for fishing, and therefore we lived pretty comfortable.

A stranger, who wished a sheep farm, then fixed upon Reef as a suitable place for that purpose. The result was that we got notice of removal from Mr Scobie, the then factor.

We had no arrears of rent, and therefore we refused in a body to do this, and stood out against it for three years, when Mr Scobie's term of office expired. We then naturally expected justice from the next factor, but on the contrary, he took up, at once, the work his predecessor had begun, and at last got us forcibly ejected.

Four families ... came to our present holding and some of the rest had to go to America. When we came here, there were no stones to be got for building a house, and as we had to turn our attention, at once, to the working of the land, which was nothing but a peat moss, we had to make temporary huts at the sea-shore to shelter us, until we got houses of turf on our lots. ...

There are now nine families on the same amount of land as was originally allowed to four. [*And the rent had been increased in the five years from over £11 to over £15.*]

We want more lands, with fair rents, fixity of tenure, with compensation for improvements, and we hope the Government will see their way to help us stock our lands and build houses, which we are willing to pay, with interest, through course of time." [22.]

CROFTERS' HOLDING ACT 1886

These and many similar revelations caused uproar, and after further agitation the Government was goaded into action. An Act was passed in 1886 which gave security of tenure to the tenant on the croft, and the right to leave the tenancy to heirs. The tenant could be evicted only if the rent became a year in arrears, for neglecting the plot, or for sub-dividing it against the regulations. On leaving the croft, the tenant could claim compensation for improvements carried out. The Crofters' Commission was set up to manage matters relating to the crofts on the estates and fix fair rents, so that immediate reductions of 50% were made.

READING THE RIOT ACT, AIGNISH 1888

RIOTS NEAR STORNOWAY, 1888

It was a great step forward, but it did not help those without land, the cottars (most were relatives to whom crofters gave space, rather than see them homeless) and squatters (on the common grazing) who, by the early 20th century, made up half of the Lewis crofting population. And it did not require that the large farms be broken up to ease the land hunger.

In the following years, 1887 and 1888, land raids took place at Park and Aignish. In Park, villagers driven by hunger raided deer reserves and a sheep farm. For this the ringleaders were sent for trial to Edinburgh, where they were acquitted; and later they were granted small crofts. A group of three hundred also petitioned for land at Galson, and several small crofts were made available. At Aignish, military and naval forces stood by when the Point crofters marched with the intention of taking over Aignish farm. Several raiders were arrested and later imprisoned. But many crofters were dissuaded at the last moment by a sympathetic, Gaelic-speaking sheriff. Later they received small holdings, suitable for fishing.

SMALL LANDOWNERS' (SCOTLAND) ACT 1911

An Act passed in 1911 set up a Scottish Land Court and permitted the compulsory purchase of land for crofts, but the difficulties of carrying this out seemed insurmountable. Trouble flared again, and continued for many years, when the soldiers returned from the First World War of 1914-18.

Early in 1919 Tong Farm was raided and the land taken over as crofts. This was followed by raids at Gress Farm, Coll Farm, Galson, Park and Stornoway. Walls were removed, croft boundaries were ploughed in the ground and, in some cases, small huts were erected.

LORD LEVERHULME

In 1918 Lewis had been bought from Lieutenant-Colonel Duncan Matheson by William Lever, Viscount Leverhulme, a successful businessman from Liverpool. He sincerely wished to turn Lewis into a viable community, and was prepared to spend considerable amounts of money to this end. But he could see no future in crofting and hoped the people would accept the large farms as a more economic way of providing the islanders with milk etc. and, instead of crofting, build up the fishing industry.

He saw the land raids as a very backward step, and stated that he would give up all his development plans for Lewis rather than give in to the raiders; but when it appeared that the Department of Agriculture for Scotland supported the raiders, Leverhulme gave up any idea of legal enforcement. At the same time, a great post-war slump caused the collapse of the continental herring market, upon which he had pinned his hopes for Lewis. And so, in 1923, he decided to give up his rights to Lewis, generously offering the whole island to its people. Although the Stornoway area was accepted under a Trust, fear of losing rights gained under the Crofting Acts led to most of the remainder of the estates being broken up and gradually sold, with most of the crofters still tenants.

It was unfortunate that a benefactor such as Lord Leverhulme and the people of Lewis should have clashed over such a fundamental issue as land. Long denied any rights over their land, the people set the greatest importance upon it, and this remained a factor which Lord Leverhulme, with his merchant's background, failed to understand. The people respected him, and he had no less regard for them; but the issue was not resolved, nor is it likely that a mutually acceptable settlement was possible in the circumstances of the time.

The slump which caused the collapse of Leverhulme's hopes for the fishing began a new wave of emigration. Two large liners, the *Metagama* and the *Marloch*, arrived in Stornoway in 1923 and 1924 and took 600 Hebrideans, mainly young men, to Canada. Other ships followed. Unlike the old forced emigrations, these were embarked upon out of necessity, but willingly, by educated young people, many of whom made names for themselves abroad.

HARRIS TWEED

In Lewis itself people found yet another outlet — the tweed industry, which flourished up to the 1960s, declined in the face of competition from man-made fibres, but can continue strongly, given good marketing.

And of course

The loom does not make the same noise
in Lewis and in Leeds:
the Lewis looms have Gaelic. [23.]

CROFTERS' ACT 1955

Crofting continued at subsistence level. An important Act of 1955 granted loans for house-building and accelerated the growth of the new, modern houses which, in all shapes and sizes, now dot the villages. The people were eager to engage in part-time work — fishing and the subsidiary industries of kippering, making fish-meal etc., weaving, building and seamanship — to support their chosen way of life. But for a time the villages were places of old people, the young and more vigorous leaving in search of larger and more dependable incomes. And young people, being curious and adventurous, will continue to leave Lewis regardless of what is offered as employment.

Yet, in recent years, it has been shown that many are eager to return if employment becomes available, such as the oil-related industry at Arnish and the pier, factory and fishing facilities at Breasclete, (though some have proved cyclical in nature) and the ever-expanding, if seasonal, tourist trade. Surveys for oil held out promise for the future (even if the promise may turn out to be a mixed blessing).

CROFTERS' REFORM ACT 1976

The Crofters' Reform Act of 1976 gave the crofters, for the first time, the option of buying their own crofts.

CROFTERS' (SCOTLAND) ACT 1993

Consolidation of the various statutes into the Crofters' (Scotland) Act of 1993 has clarified current crofting law, and debate has centred recently on community ownership, by the local crofters, of the land itself and its resources, while also retaining protection under the Crofting Acts. Perhaps we may yet see crofting as not only a chosen way of life but one with reasonable returns, though many seem willing to forego this for the other, deeper satisfactions which the life offers.

Lewis

That, surely, is the main imprint which the crofting generations, a truly classless society, have left on Lewis. Throughout all their struggles, sorrows and oppression, they steadfastly held on to ideals of what was worthwhile. Thought of financial gain has certainly not been foremost in crofting. And in an essentially materialistic age this is a quality to value.

Sitting there
on the side of the hill,
with the snipe passing by,
a swoop in the eternity of Lewis,
you were at peace,
your cattle close at hand
and the day long,
the gentle air in your nostrils
and Barvas Hills on the farthest horizon. [24.]

12.

SIR ALEXANDER MACKENZIE

Alexander Mackenzie was born in Stornoway in 1764 in Luskentyre House, where Martin's Memorial Church stands today. At the age of ten he emigrated with his family to New York. His father, Kenneth Mackenzie of Melbost, fought in the American War of Independence on the side of the King and Alexander was sent to Canada for safety in 1778.

A year later, at the age of fifteen, he joined the Toronto office of one of the partners of the North-West Fur Company, which had developed as a rival to the famous Hudson Bay Company. By his twenties he had shown such enterprise that he was sent to oversee the company's richest fur area near Lake Athabasca, with the aim of further exploration of this vast unknown territory.

It was here that he decided to search for a route to the Pacific Ocean and be the first European to cross the North American Continent from coast to coast. In 1789 he set out, with twelve companions in five canoes, from the head of Lake Athabasca. They sailed North on the Slave River, through the Great Slave Lake, and found the river which now bears his name. They continued through swarms of mosquitoes westwards to the Rocky Mountains, where the river turned north, entered Eskimo country and finally reached, not the Pacific, but the Arctic Ocean.

He had followed the course of the river now called Mackenzie (which he actually named Disappointment); but, although determined to try again, he had to turn back in a race against winter. He then began to prepare for another attempt, studying geography and surveying and collecting instruments to aid his plans. Finally he was ready. This time he followed the Peace River out of Lake Athabasca, but that became full of rapids and dangerous at the approach to the Rocky Mountains and then petered out. They carried the canoes overland and found the Fraser River, which did not, however, promise a route west. It was decided to stow the canoes and continue on foot.

After fifteen days they reached the Pacific Ocean. And there on a rock he painted 'Alexander Mackenzie, from Canada by land, 22nd July, 1793'. He was named as the first European to cross the North American Continent from coast to coast, and he was knighted for his achievement. In 1805 he returned to Scotland, where he married Geddes Mackenzie, and he lived on her estates in Inverness-shire until his death in 1820.

THE FLANNAN ISLES MYSTERY

Just before Christmas 1900 the light of the new (barely a year old) lighthouse on the Flannan Isles, west of Lewis, mysteriously ceased to shine. After investigation it was found that all three keepers had disappeared without trace. It was thought that they had been victims of a huge Atlantic breaker, but nothing has ever been proved.

Though three men dwelt on Flannan Isle
To keep the lamp alight,
As we steered under the lee, we caught
No glimmer through the night...

Aye; though we hunted high and low,
And hunted everywhere,
Of the three men's fate we found no trace
Of any kind in any place
But a door ajar, and an untouched meal,
And an overtoppled chair. [25.]

THE *IOLAIRE* DISASTER

On New Year's Day, 1919, there occurred the most tragic disaster that Lewis has had to bear in recent times — the wrecking of the *Iolaire* on the rocks of the 'Beasts of Holm', within sight of Stornoway, with the loss of more than 200 men, mainly sailors, returning from the First World War. *Iolaire* is the Gaelic word for 'eagle'. The broken wings of this eagle brought a terrible grief:

After the war had said its last
and they were sailing into frantic arms —
to have been stunned by their own Lewis seas!
One cannot speak of this
or ask the illuminating storms
to write their reason on a plain coast. [26.]

The book *Call na h-Iolaire* is a Gaelic account of the disaster by Tormod Calum Dòmhnallach (Norman Malcolm Macdonald), and it includes a summary in English.

THE TOWN OF STORNOWAY

The favourable area of Stornoway, with its relatively good soil and sheltered bay, was settled from earliest times. There are Neolithic chambered cairns near Stornoway. From being a small farming and fishing community it became a landing-stage for the Viking longships on their raids, and then a Norse settlement.

Stornoway Castle, the Macleod stronghold, stood on a rocky islet protecting the inner harbour. Early in the 16th century it was besieged and captured by the Earl of Huntly. It was later used again by the Macleods as a base against the Fife Adventurers, but it was finally battered down by Cromwell's troops, who then built a fort to guard the harbour. Though nothing of that remains, a ground plan is held at

STORNOWAY COAT OF ARMS

Worcester College, Oxford. But Stornoway Castle exists only as rubble beneath Stornoway's quays. The present Lews Castle was built in Victorian times by Sir James Matheson of Sutherland, who had made a fortune in the Far East and who bought Lewis in 1844.

Beside Stornoway Castle a small town grew up, expanding along what is now Cromwell Street and Bayhead Street and down the outer harbour to Newton Street. The market, which received cattle from all areas, was outside Stornoway, near the present-day War Memorial. During the 18th century the thatched 'black houses' (some of which were inhabited into the second half of the 20th century in the country districts) began to be replaced by houses of stone and lime.

The 1850s population movements and the later growth of the fishing industry, led to Stornoway's rapid expansion. Tenements, houses and hotels spread, following the plans of the old fields and tracks; and the quays were greatly improved by Sir James Matheson.

It is said that before this, around 1830, Lewis was the scene of the fearful exploits of *Mac an t-Srònaich*, who is thought to have murdered at least twelve people in a reign of terror lasting over two years; and up to very recent times children tiptoed fearfully past a dark and gloomy cavern in the grounds of Lews Castle which was known as *Mac an t-Srònaich's* cave, and which still held the aura of horror of that time long before.

In 1873 the Nicolson Institute School was founded by a bequest from Alexander Morison Nicolson, a local man whose enterprise had gained him wealth in shipping before he was killed by a ship's boiler explosion at the early age of thirty-three. The school was later endowed by his brothers and by Sir James Matheson. Before this, education was largely in the hands of the Church, with the help of the Gaelic School Societies. And the Lewis young people's will to achieve in their education has been strong and their successes notable.

Stornoway is now a bustling centre with a population of about 6,000, and with lively and thriving cultural activities. Stornoway is the stepping-off point for all the country districts of Lewis and is itself situated amid beautiful countryside and seascapes — a true island capital.

THE NATURAL HERITAGE

As we follow the prints from the past, we discover not only the island's history and pre-history, but also a very rich natural heritage, because the Lewis hills, moors, lochs, shores, surrounding seas and islets are very important habitats for an amazing variety of wildlife.

The outlying Shiant Isles, together with the National Nature Reserves of North Rona and St Kilda, with St Kilda, in fact, designated as a World Heritage Site, are especially important breeding sites for many kinds of seabirds, among these being the gannet, guillemot and puffin.

Minke whales, dolphins and porpoises are among the many species in the sea channel of the Minch, with populations of otters near the coasts, and with large numbers of grey seals, breeding colonies of which include those in the Sound of Harris and on North Rona.

Coastal salt marshes such as those at Gress and Tong, provide important wintering, breeding and feeding sites for wildfowl, and for waders such as snipe and oystercatchers. Among the birds of moor and loch are the grouse, cuckoo and wheatear. The extensive mixed woodland surrounding Lews Castle, Stornoway, provides habitats for many birds, especially rooks and herons.

In summer and early autumn, the island is graced by the many-coloured flowers of wild plants, among them the delicate purple pink of spotted wild orchids, the bright yellow of tormentil, birds-foot trefoil and, in damp areas, iris and marsh marigolds, with later the purple of heather and thistles.

STORNOWAY C. 1853

Nature conservation in the Outer Hebrides, as elsewhere, is designed to preserve the fragile ecological balance, and protect from harmful development sites of geology, flora and fauna of special scientific interest (SSSIs). Most of the areas noted above come into this category, which also includes the geology of Port of Ness and Tolsta Head, and the fen and marine environment of Loch Dalbeg on the west coast. Development in other areas must also prove that it is sustainable and does not prejudice the needs of future generations through heedless destruction of the natural heritage. Over-development, pollution, litter and general lack of care endanger the natural environment and its wildlife. Only by taking an active part in environmental conservation can we play our part in their protection.

We have travelled the Island down many ages. This, then, is Lewis — solid as its ancient stone, stormy or sun-dazzled, with a heritage of great value to explore and wonder about, and with prints from the past everywhere to be found, possibly most of all in the Gaelic language. To end, here are Gaelic poems by Ruaraidh MacThòmais (Derick Thomson), and Anna Frater They are given in the original Gaelic and in translation.

WHEN I COME BACK

When I come back
the potato flowers will be out,
the bees humming,
the cows lowing to milking
when I come back.

When I arrive,
shaking you by the hand,
the coldness of the ring
will be on the palm of hope
when I arrive.

When I lie down
in your kind breast,
the cuckoo will come
and wailing with it,
when I lie down.

And when I rise
on that morning,
the ring will be shattered
and the cow dry
and the dark brown island as I first knew it.

NUAIR A THILLEAS MI

Nuair a thilleas mi
bidh 'm bàrr-gùg air a bhuntàt',
bidh 'n t-seillean a' crònan,
bidh bhò a' muathal gu eadradh
nuair a thilleas mi.

Nuair a ruigeas mi,
a' breith air làimh oirbh,
bidh fuachd na fàinne
air deàrn an dòchais
nuair a ruigeas mi.

Nuair a laigheas mi
an com do charthannais,
thig an gug-gùg
's an o-draochan maille ris
an uair a laigheas mi.

'S an uair a dh'èireas mi
air a' mhadainn ud,
bidh 'n fhàinne sgealbt'
is a' bhò gun bhainn' aice,
's an t-eilean riabhach mar bu chiad aithne dhomh. [27.]

TWO ROADS

Why should I follow
the long, smooth, straight road?
Although the road I take is crooked
and the stones cut my feet
and climbing the hill
leaves me breathless
I am not confronted
by the same prospect
day after day.
And up on the hill
I can see around me,
I can see that there is more in store for me
than a straight, long, smooth road.
You keep your eyes fixed on one point
right in front of you -
and you cannot see
that the world is changing around you.

DA RATHAD

Carson a bu chòir dhomh gabhail
na slighe ceart, lom, fada?
Ged a tha an rathad air a bheil mi càm
agus tha na clachan a' gearradh mo chasan,
agus tha dìreadh an leothaid
gam fhàgail gun anail,
chan e an aon rud
a tha mise coimhead romham
latha an dèidh latha.
Agus shuas air an leathad
chì mi timcheall orm,
chì mi gu bheil barrachd ann dhòmhs'
na slighe cheart, fhada, lom.
Tha thusa a' cumail do shùilean air an aon rud
ceart, dìreach air do bheulaibh -
agus chan fhaic thu gu bheil an saoghal
ag atharrachadh timcheall ort. [28.]

REFERENCES

1. Lines from a boatman's song quoted in *Wonder Tales from Scottish Myth and Legend* by Donald A. Mackenzie (Blackie & Sons, London, 1920).

2. 'Cet and Conall', from the 8th century Irish Saga *Scéla Mucce Meic Dá Thó*, translated by Gerard Murphy. Quoted in *Poetry Australia*, No.63, May 1977 (South Head Press, New South Wales).

3. Part of a translation of 'Am Beannachadh Bealltain' (The Beltane Blessing), from Volume I of *Carmina Gadelica* by Alexander Carmichael (1900-71, six volumes, published by Scottish Academic Press).

4. A translation of 'Manaidh' (Omens), from Volume II of *Carmina Gadelica*.

5. Part of 'Cù Chulainn's Lament over Ferdia' from *The Táin*, Thomas Kinsella's translation of the Irish epic *Táin Bó Cuailgne*. Quoted in *Poetry Australia*, No.63.

6. Part of a translation of a lament for Fionn by Ossian, from *Heroic Poetry from the Book of the Dean of Lismore*, edited by Neil Ross (Oliver & Boyd, Edinburgh, 1939).

7. Part of a translation of 'Thàinig na Cait Oirnn' (The Cats are Come on Us), from Volume IV of *Carmina Gadelica*. The Cats were Norsemen from the very north of Scotland (*Cataibh* is the Gaelic for Sutherland).

8. From 'Music in the Home Life of the Gael' by Alexander Macdonald, from Volume XXXIII (1925-27) of *Transactions of the Gaelic Society of Inverness*.

9. Part of the Harlaw 'Brosnachadh Catha' (Incitement to Battle), translated by Derick Thomson and quoted in his book *An Introduction to Gaelic Poetry* (Gollancz, 1974).

10. From Robert Bain's *History of Ross, the County Palatine of Scotland* (Pefferside Press, Dingwall, 1889).

11. A verse from a translation of 'Oran do MhacLeòid Dhùn Bheagain' (A Song to MacLeod of Dunvegan) by Ruairidh MacMhuirich (Roderick Morison), *An Clàrsair Dall* (The Blind Harper), from *An Clàrsair Dall* (The Blind Harper), edited by William Matheson (Scottish Gaelic Texts Society, 1970).

12. The opening of the second section of *Beinn Dorain*, Iain Crichton Smith's translation of the poem by Duncan Bàn Macintyre (Akros Publications, 1969, Ratcliffe on Trent, Nottingham).

13. Verses from a translation by Harold Boulton of 'Eilean an Fhraoich' (Isle of the Heather) by Murdo MacLeod, from Volume III of *Songs of the North* (J.B. Cromer & Co. Ltd., 139 Bond Street, London W1, 1935).

14. 'Tha Thu air Aigeann M'inntinn' (You are at the Bottom of My Mind) by Iain Mac a' Ghobhainn (Iain Crichton Smith), translated by the author in his collection *Bìobuill is Sanasan-Reice* (Gairm, 1965).

15. 'Do Charaid' (For a Friend) by Dòmhnall MacAmhlaigh (Donald MacAulay), translated by the author, from the anthology *Honour'd Shade,* edited by Norman MacCaig (W. & R. Chambers, 1959).

16. 'Bùrn is Mòine 's Coirc' (Water and Peats and Oats) by Ruaraidh MacThòmais (Derick Thomson), translated by the author in his collected poems, *Creachadh na Clàrsaich / Plundering the Harp* (Macdonald Publishers, Loanhead, Midlothian, 1982).

17. 'Reothairt' (Spring Tide) by Somhairle MacGill-Eain (Sorley MacLean), translated by the author in his Collected Poems, *O Choille gu Bearradh /From Wood to Ridge* (Carcanet, 1989)

18. Part of a poem about Dalmore by Roderick M. Stephen, from the *Eilean an Fhraoich Annual* (Stornoway Gazette, 1967).

19. 'Do Mo Mhàthair' (To My Mother), from *Bìobuill is Sanasan-Reice.*

20. From the *Royal Commission Report on the Highlands and Islands and evidence taken by H.M. Commissioners of Enquiry into the conditions of Crofters and Cottars in the Highlands and Islands of Scotland in 1883,* XXXII, published in 1884 and printed by Neill & Co., Edinburgh.

21. From the *Royal Commission Report,* XXXII.

22. From the *Royal Commission Report,* XXXIV.

23. 'Ceòl na Beairte' (The Music of the Loom), from *Creachadh na Clàrsaich.*

24. 'Cliathaich a' Chnuic' (The Side of the Hill), from *Creachadh na Clàrsaich.*

25. From 'Flannan Isle' by Wilfred Wilson Gibson, from *Rhyme and Reason,* an anthology edited by Raymond O'Malley and Denys Thomson (Chatto Educational, 1970).

26. From 'After the War' by Iain Crichton Smith, from his collection *Thistles and Roses* (Eyre and Spottiswoode, 1961).

27. 'Nuair a Thilleas Mi' (When I Come Back), from *Creachadh na Clàrsaich.*

28. Dà Rathad Two Roads, from *Fon t-Slige,* (Under the Shell), by Anna Frater (Gairm, 1995).

MORE REFERENCE MATERIAL

HMSO:

Royal Commission on the Ancient and Historical Monuments of Scotland: *Ninth Report with Inventory of Monuments and Constructions in the Outer Hebrides, Skye and the Small Isles,* 1928.
Graham Ritchie and Mary Harman, *Argyll and the Western Isles,* 1985.
Joanna Close-Brooks, *The Highlands,* 1987.
John M Baxter and Michael B Usher, Ed., *The Islands of Scotland: A Living Marine Heritage,* 1994.

HISTORIC SCOTLAND, HISTORIC BUILDINGS AND MONUMENTS, AN EXECUTIVE AGENCY OF THE SECRETARY OF STATE FOR SCOTLAND:
Anna Ritchie, *Scotland BC,* 1988.
Anna Ritchie, *Picts,* 1989.
Anna Ritchie and David J. Breeze, *An Introduction to the Archaeology of the Romans, Scots, Angles and Vikings,* 1991.
Noel Fojut, Denys Pringle and Bruce Walker, *Monuments of the Western Isles,* 1994.
Alexander Fenton, *The Island Blackhouse,* 1989.

NATIONAL MUSEUMS OF SCOTLAND:
Jenni Calder, *The Story of the Scottish Soldier* 1600-1914, 1987.

Ordnance Survey Maps showing visible antiquities:
1:50 000 Second Series (three maps to cover Lewis).
1:25 000 Second Series (requiring more maps).
Ordnance Survey, 32 Romsey Road, Maybush, Southampton, SO9 4DH.

Patrick Ashmore, *Calanais: The Standing Stones,* Urras nan Turachan Ltd., 1995.

Ian Armit, Ed., *Beyond The Brochs,* Edinburgh University Press, 1990.

Michael Taylor, *The Lewis Chessmen,* British Museum Publications, 1978.

Genealogies of the Macleod Barons of Lewis, in *Burke's Landed Gentry,* 1937.

Genealogies of the Mackenzie Earls of Seaforth, in *The Complete Peerage,* Volume XI, G.H.White, 1949.

Donald MacAulay, Ed., *Nua-bhàrdachd Ghàidhlig/Modern Scottish Gaelic Poems,* Canongate books Ltd., 1995.¡

Robin Bell, Ed., *The Best of Scottish Poetry*, Chambers, 1989.

Donald Macdonald, *Lewis: a History of the Island*, Gordon Wright Publishing, 1978.

James Hunter, *The Making of the Crofting Community*, John Donald Publishers Ltd., 1976.

T. M. Devine, *The Great Highland Famine*, John Donald Publishers Ltd., 1988.

John Munro Mackenzie, *Diary 1851*, Acair, 1994.

I.M.M. Macphail, *The Crofters' War*, Acair, 1989.

Angus M. Macdonald, *A Lewis Album*, Edited by Sheila Macleod, Acair, 1982.

Francis Thompson, *The Hebrides in Old Picture Postcards*, European Library, 1989.

Bilingual Education in the Western Isles, Scotland, 1975-1981, Report by John Murray and Catherine Morrison, Acair, 1984.

THE EXHIBITS

As well as the many sites of antiquities in Lewis, there is a preserved 'black house' at Arnol, and others at Garenin, a visitors' centre and exhibition at Callanish, and a Norse-type mill at Shawbost. Several Local History Societies have also set up exhibitions, and these bring alive again the traditional island way of life, which is fast fading under modern influences.

Many of the finds from Lewis can be seen on display in Museum nan Eilean in Stornoway, and also in mainland museums such as the National Museum of Antiquities, in Edinburgh. The fine Norse brooches and many items of value can be seen in Stornoway. The museums make available to us these fascinating prints from the past — our heritage.

Other comparatively recent noteworthy Lewis finds include:

A Neolithic axe, comprising a stone axehead in a wooden haft, from Shulishader, discovered in 1983, and radiocarbon dated to about 3,500-3,000 BC.

A Bronze Age organic object, possibly a boot lining, consisting of a mat of cattle hair, with plaited horsehair cord and twisted woollen cords attached, found at Sheshader in 1991, and radiocarbon dated to about 1,300-840 BC.

A Viking hacksilver hoard, comprising about 40 pieces of hacksilver, originally buried in a cow's horn, and found in the grounds of Lews Castle, Stornoway, 1988-1990. Two fragments from two Norman derniers date the hoard to 1000-1050 AD.

Experts have noted the organic Lewis finds to be amongst the finest and most interesting discovered. If not properly conserved, however, these rare objects may disintegrate, and it is essential to notify local or national museums of the locations of any finds, so that such priceless relics of the past can be safeguarded.

Several important archaeological excavations have recently taken place in Lewis and in the Uists. The Lewis sites include a broch near Berie Sands, Uig, which reveals evidence of four phases of occupation over a period of a thousand years from the Iron Age; there is a dun located at nearby Loch Baravat, which has produced a wealth of finds, many underwater, including part of a large basket or creel which is two thousand years old but is identical in form to creels which were in use very recently in Lewis; and there is an Iron Age settlement at Bosta Beach on the island of Great Bernera.

Unfortunately, many sites threatened by coastal erosion have been neglected, and funds to initiate urgent rescue operations are required now if precious finds are to be saved. Many of these areas could then be included in tourism ventures which, by helping the Island economy, would benefit everyone.